GOOGLE ADS MANAGEMENT

How to manage your ads like a pro

Mike Ncube

Copyright © 2022 by Mike Ncube

All rights reserved. No part of this book may be used or reproduced by any means, graphic, electronic, or mechanical, including photocopying, recording, taping, or by any information storage retrieval system, without the written permission of the publisher except in the case of brief quotations embodied in critical articles and reviews.

INTRODUCTION

Google Ads is a leading advertising platform that's helping millions of businesses around the globe to connect with their customers, clients, donors, volunteers, and many others they want to reach online.

Using Search tools, they are reaching them at those important moments when they want to buy, learn, download, go somewhere or take any other action that is important to them.

But it doesn't end there. Google Ads has a plethora of campaigns and tools to reach audiences across the internet in its vast Display and Video networks that reach over 90% of internet users.

And the power of these networks can be seen in the precise targeting options that are available, like targeting people based on their lifestyles, demographics, interests, buyer stage, keyword choices and many other options.

As an advertiser who uses Google Ads, however, all this can be confusing and for some can be just too much to take it all in. In fact, Google Ads is such a large platform that you won't need many of the features, controls, and campaigns depending on the nature of your business.

What is important is that you focus on the core features that will make a difference to your business, organisation, learning plan or whatever your primary goals in Google Ads are.

So, what will you learn in this book? This is an important question, and the answer begins with why I wrote this book in the first place.

Firstly, as a Google Ads specialist with over 13 years' experience, I've worked with almost every type of business out there and there is barely anything new that I see these days.

So, I've put some of the most important management tactics and tips that I've learnt and used over the years in this book. You get to see some tricks that leading pay per click (PPC) specialists use to manage their campaigns and achieve a great return on ad spend.

I'm confident that by the time you complete this book, you'll have a good understanding of Google Ads and how to manage your campaigns or client's campaigns effectively.

Mike Ncube
Google Ads specialist

Who this book is for

This book is for anyone that wants to run effective campaigns and make Google Ads a highly profitable channel for their business or organisation. This includes:

- Business owners that run their own campaigns and want to learn how to do it effectively.
- Entrepreneurs who want to setup multiple campaigns and scale their businesses.
- Marketers that are new to Google Ads and want to learn the features and controls and run effective ads.

People who are new to pay per click (PPC) advertising in Google Ads and want to learn this platform.

Contents

Introduction To Google Ads Management 1
   Have a sufficient budget 1
   Pick the right campaign goal 2
   Target the search partners 3
   Regularly check search terms report 4
   Check the assets report 4
   Conduct more keyword research 5
   Add negative keywords 5
   Update text ads 5
   Use a Google audience solution 6
   Update your bid strategy 7
   Use the performance planner 7

Chapter 1: Bid Strategy 8
   Automated bidding 8
   Maximise clicks 9
      When to use 9
   Maximise conversions 10
      When to use 10
   Target cost per action (CPA) 10
      When to use 11
   Maximise conversion value 11
      When to use 12
   Target return on ad spend 12
      When to use 13
   Target impression share 13
      When to use 14

Enhanced CPC.. 14
   When to use.. 14
Manual bidding 15
Manual CPC... 15
   When to use.. 15
Using Google Ads' automated bidding 16
Awareness-based bidding strategies................................ 17
   When to use.. 18
Consideration-focused bidding strategies....................... 18
   When to use.. 19
Conversion-focused bidding strategies 19
   When to use.. 20
Revenue-focused bidding strategies................................ 21
   When to use.. 21
Which Google Ads bid strategy is right for your goal(s)?. 21
   Increase Clicks 22
   Increase impressions and awareness 23
   Increase conversions and conversion value 23
Google Ads' bidding best practices 24
   Start with an automated strategy 24
   Don't overbid... 25
   Update low ranked keywords 26

Chapter 2: Budgets 27

Advertising budget... 27
   Search campaign 28
   Shopping campaign 28
   Display campaign 28
   Remarketing campaign 29
   YouTube video campaign 29
Cost per click 29
Business goals.. 30

- Type of business 31
- Company size 31
- Other factors to consider when setting your budget 32
  - Start with a test budget 32
  - What are your goals for leads or sales?.......................... 33
  - Check keyword volumes 33
  - What is a suggested bid?... 34
  - Check competitors 35
- 14 savvy ways to spend any leftover in your Google Ads budget 36
  - Move your leftover budget to another campaign 36
  - Create a shared budget 36
  - Add more keywords 37
  - Add broad match types.. 37
  - Promote more products or services 38
  - Increase ad positions... 38
  - Target other locations 38
  - Update ad scheduling 38
  - Include search partners 39
  - Target the Display Network 39
  - Set up a remarketing campaign 40
  - Use bid modifiers 40
  - Target people outside your location 41
  - Target all device types... 41
- What's a good Google Ads budget for a small business? 42
  - Level of competition 42
  - Average CPC.. 43
  - Impressions and click volumes.. 44
  - Desired ad positions 44
  - Conversion targets.. 45
- Setting your Google Ads budget 45
- Minimum Google Ads budget... 47
- Google Ad costs... 48

Is Google Ads always expensive at the beginning? 50

Chapter 3: Click Through Rate (CTR) 53
Ad position 53
Ad relevance 54
Bids 54
Search terms 55
Benefits of improving CTRs 55
    Gain top positions 56
    Remove low CTR keywords 57
    Remove low CTR search terms 57
    Remove low CTR ads 58
    Add ad extensions 58
    Include keywords in the text ad 59
    Make ads relevant 59
    Ad extensions 60
What's a good CTR for a Google Ad? 61
    Below 1% CTR 61
    Between 1-5% CTR 62
    Above 5% CTR 62
    Above 10% CTR 63
    20%+ CTR 63
Why it's important to have a high CTR in Google Ads 64
    Helps achieve good quality scores 65
    Increases website traffic 65
    Improves conversions 65
    Achieves higher rankings 66
What is an average CTR in Google Ads? 66
    Search campaign CTR 67
    Search term CTR vs keyword CTR 67

Chapter 4: Conversion Tracking 69
Why Google Ads conversion tracking is not working 71

- Conversion tracking not set up 71
  - Tracking code not installed 72
  - Installed in the wrong place 72
  - Conversions not imported 73
- How to setup offline conversion tracking in Google Ads. 73
  - How it works 74
  - Conversions from clicks 74
  - Conversions from calls 74
- How to set up Google Ads conversion tracking 75
  - Link Google Ads & Analytics 75
  - Import goals into Google Ads 75
  - Update settings 76
  - Category 76
  - Value 76
  - Conversion window 76
  - Attribution model 76
  - Update columns 77
- The differences between Google Ads and Analytics conversion tracking 77
  - Set up templates 78
  - Tracking code setup 79
  - Reporting 79
  - Multi-channel funnels 80

Chapter 5: Cost Per Click (CPC) 82
- Campaign type 82
- Text ads 84
- Keywords 84
- Bid strategy 85
- What is the average CPC in Google Ads? 86
- Industry type 87
- Sector type 88
- Campaign type 88

Keyword type 89
Lower keyword bids 90
Add negative keywords 91
Change bidding strategy 92
Improve quality scores 94
Find long tail keywords 95
Use broad match type keywords 96

Chapter 6: Keyword Research 97
  Setting up a successful PPC campaign 97
    Find good keywords 98
    Estimation of traffic volumes 98
    Estimation of costs 99
    Discover competitors' strategy 99
  How to use the Google keyword research tool 100
    Add up to three keywords 100
    Add a landing page 101
    Choose the location 101
    Check the recommendations tab 102
    Use the forecasting tool 102
  How many keywords should you have in each ad group? 103
    A minimum five keywords 103
    Maximum 20 keywords 104
    Follow the rule of two 104

Chapter 7: Landing Pages 106
  Why use PPC landing pages? 107
  PPC landing pages for Google Ads 107
  PPC landing pages bounce rates 108
  What factors make up landing page quality score in Google Ads? 109

Fast loading pages 110
Fully mobile-responsive pages 110
Bounce rate 110
Website content 111
Ways to improve your Google Ads landing pages 111
Avoid popups 112
Remove all distractions 112
Add a call to action 113
Use software like Hotjar 114
Use white space 114
Add reviews 115
Have an 'About Us' page 115
Add a contact form 116
Have a 'Thank you' page 116
Update your footer 117

Chapter 8: Match Types 118

Broad match 118

Phrase match 119

Exact match 119

Which keyword match types should I use in Google Ads? 119

Broad match 120
Phrase match 121
Exact Match 122

Chapter 9: Negative Keywords 123

Keyword Planner tool 124

Search terms report 125

Brainstorming 125

When to add negative keywords in Google Ads 126

Keyword research 126
Campaign launch 126

Campaign management 127
7 reasons why you should add negative keywords........ 127
    Reducing wasted budget.. 128
    Increased conversion rates... 128
    Increased sales for targeted keywords 129
    Reduced cost per conversion.. 129
    Improved click through rates 129
    Reduced bounce rates 130
    Increased profitability.. 130

Chapter 10: Quality Scores 131
    Quality score facts... 131
    It is based on exact match keywords 131
    It contributes to ad rank 132
    It is a diagnostic tool 132
    It is a keyword metric.. 132
    It is not a key performance indicator 132
    It is calculated at auction time.. 133
    It should be improved 133
    It is affected by the landing page experience................ 133
    It is affected by expected CTR 134
    It is affected by ad relevance 134
    Not an account or campaign metric 134
    New keywords have null quality scores 134
    Check historical quality scores 135
    How you structure your account doesn't matter 135
    Running ads on another network doesn't matter 135
    Your ad position doesn't affect quality scores 136
    You don't need to bid higher to improve quality scores..... 136
    Have 3-5 ads per ad group to improve quality scores 136
    Add dynamic keyword insertion in ads........................... 136
    The user's device is important.. 137
How important is a quality score? 137
What's a good keyword quality score? 138
    Low quality score... 139

Average quality score 139
　　　Good quality score 140
　　　Excellent quality score 140
　How to check keyword quality score in Google Ads 140
　　　Check keywords status column 140
　　　Quality score status columns 141
　　　Historical quality score status columns 142
　5 tips to improve keyword quality scores....................... 143
　　　Improve landing pages 144
　　　Increase click through rate 146
　　　Make ads relevant 147
　　　Add ad extensions 148
　　　Target the right search terms 148
　How to get 10/10 quality scores.. 149
　　　Improve expected click through rate (CTR) 150
　　　Improve ad relevance 151
　　　Improve landing page experience 151
　　　Add ad extensions 152
　　　Remove low performing search terms 152
　Will paused keywords affect quality scores? 153

Chapter 11: Remarketing...154
　Audience sources 155
　　　Google Ads tag 155
　　　Google Analytics 155
　　　YouTube 155
　　　Customer Data 156
　Audience lists 156
　Audience Insights 156
　Which advanced remarketing services to set up 157
　　　Dynamic remarketing 158
　　　Remarketing lists for search ads (RLSA) 158
　　　YouTube remarketing 158
　How to setup PPC remarketing.. 159

    Link Google Ads & Analytics 159
    Create an audience in Analytics 160
    Create new image ads 162
    Max file size 162
    Create a PPC remarketing campaign 163

Conclusion **164**

Resources **165**

About The Author **167**

Introduction To Google Ads Management

Effective PPC campaign management is what every Google Ads account needs to be able to achieve a good return on ad spend (ROAS).

When you set up your campaign, you will leave it to run for a period, like a few days or a few weeks, depending on the volume of traffic you get. But you will, at a certain point, need to check what results you've had, and which search queries have driven clicks to your website.

Based on your findings, you will start your PPC campaign management to improve metrics such as conversions, conversion rate, click through rate (CTR) and more.

Here is a summary of PPC campaign management tips which we will be covering in this book:

Have a sufficient budget

Your budget should be at least 10 times your target cost per acquisition (tCPA) bid strategy. For other bid strategies, aim to have at least 20-30% more budget than your average daily spend. With a sufficient budget, this helps the machine learning algorithm to find new search recommendations that convert at a higher rate, and combined with broad match keywords, you will reach a broader audience of targeted customers.

Also, check the campaign budget simulator to see weekly estimates for your new daily budget and explore how that can impact your search traffic and your conversions. To see the campaign budget simulator, go to the campaign page in your account and next to your campaign, under the budget column, you can see it by moving your mouse over the icon next to your daily budgeted amount.

Campaign	Budget
Art Therapy Course	£130.00/day
Remarketing	£5.00/day

Pick the right campaign goal

At the campaign setup level, you will have several goal types to choose from. These goals include sales, leads, website traffic, brand awareness and more. Your choice between these will determine where your ads appear and who gets to see them. This also determines how you manage your campaign based on the reports that you are viewing. If you want to run a search campaign for example, you have the sales, leads or website traffic to choose from. If you are a retailer, you will be able to see how many sales you are getting and metrics like conversion rate and cost per conversion will be important to you as you carry out your PPC campaign management.

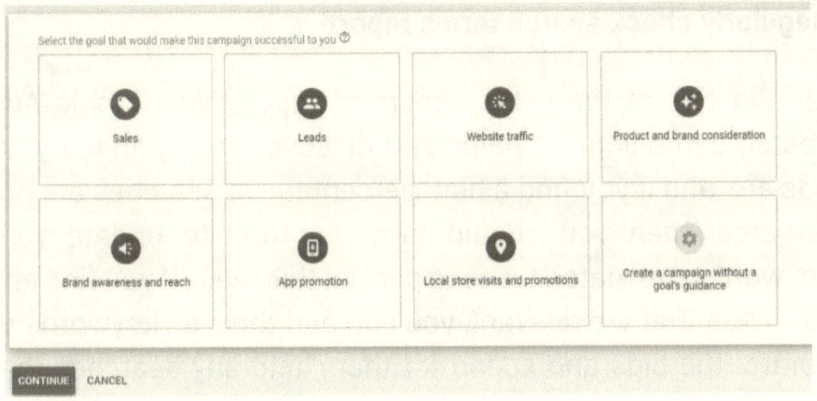

Target the search partners

Many advertisers choose to advertise on the Google.com search engine only and miss out on a potentially receptive audience within its search partners. These partners include hundreds of websites that utilise search technology and this includes some of Google's own properties like Play, YouTube, Maps and more. By default, when creating a new campaign, your ads are opted into the Search Network, but you can remove this and add it later to see how it performs for your products or sales. At the campaign level, you can segment your traffic by 'network' and see how the search partners are doing for you.

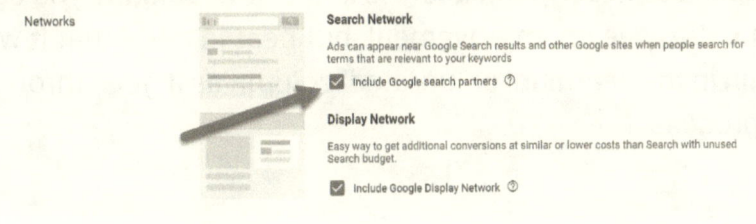

Regularly check search terms report

This is one of the most important reports for Google Ads search campaigns. It helps you discover how targeted your ads are, and if you find a high percentage of searches are not targeted, then you should take the time to update your keywords and match types to correct this. Also, if you find any searches that are relevant, you can add them as keywords to control the bids and spend for them, and any searches that are not relevant, you should add as negative keywords at the campaign or ad group level.

Check the assets report

This is a search campaign report that shows how each of your headline and description assets are performing at auction time. The performance rating section has four columns that reveal the status of each asset: best, good, low, and unrated. This is a percentage score that helps you decide how you need to improve the asset, or if it is in the 'best' column, then nothing else needs to be done. For each asset, you can also see how many search campaigns are using that and you can click the link to see the list of ads. If, for example, a headline or description asset is in the 'low' column, you can update it to see an improvement, but bear in mind that it will remain in the 'learning' or 'unrated' column as it goes through this process.

	Performance rating				
	Best	Good	Low	Learning	Unrated
	0.00%	0.00%	0.00%	0.00%	100.00%
	0.00%	0.00%	0.00%	0.00%	100.00%
	0.00%	0.00%	0.00%	0.00%	100.00%
	0.00%	53.91%	0.00%	0.00%	46.09%
	0.00%	47.09%	0.00%	0.00%	52.91%
	0.00%	100.00%	0.00%	0.00%	0.00%

Conduct more keyword research

Regular keyword research is an important exercise to find new keyword and search phrase recommendations. Google Ads has the Keyword Planner tool that you can find in the 'Tools & Settings' section.

Add negative keywords

Negative keywords block searches that are not relevant to your business, from triggering your ads. Check your search terms report regularly – once or twice a week – and when you find searches that are not relevant, add them as negative keywords.

Update text ads

Part of your PPC management tasks should include updating your responsive search ads. This includes checking the

'Recommendations' tab to see if there are any recommendations to improve the headlines and descriptions in your ads. Doing so helps to improve the ad targeting as the system has more to choose from and to use them at auction time. The context of the search determines which headlines and descriptions appear and providing more of these help your ads reach the right users and rewards you with good quality scores.

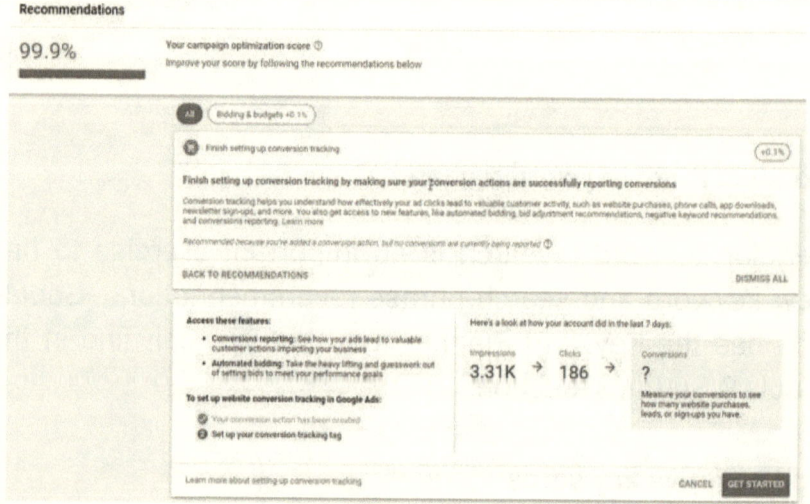

Use a Google audience solution

If you have some broad keywords that you want to target but are not sure if you will see positive results, then you can layer an audience of people that are in the market for what you sell. You can layer audience solutions on your campaigns or ad groups like Affinity and In-market audiences, and you have hundreds to choose from in your account.

Update your bid strategy

Part of your PPC campaign management should include testing out different bid strategies. There are four bid strategy types that you can use depending on your goals: awareness-based, conversion-focused, consideration-focused, and revenue-focused. If you want to increase awareness for your products or services for example, you will use the target impression share bid strategy to get as many impressions as possible for your budget. If you want to increase conversions, you can start with the maximise conversions bid strategy and then change to Target cost per conversion (CPA) as you get more conversion data.

Use the performance planner

Use this tool to plan your campaigns over the next few months. This allows you to set the optimal budgets and bids to achieve the goals you want to achieve, like the number of clicks or conversions that you want each month. Google recommends that you run this tool every month and upload the suggestions to your campaigns to achieve the targets.

CHAPTER 1

Bid Strategy

Google Ads' bidding strategies are an important part of advertising on Google. They help determine where your ads appear, how much you'll pay for each click, how competitive your ads are, what budget to set and much more.

So, setting a bid strategy is an important part of setting up a Google Ads campaign and managing it. as you do so, you'll often have to change from one bid strategy to another as you promote your products or services.

There are several ways to set your bids. You can set an individual bidding strategy at the campaign level, or you can set a portfolio bidding strategy at the account level and apply it to multiple campaigns in your account.

In this section, I list all the Google Ads bidding strategies available to you that you can use in your search, display, remarketing, video, and other campaign types.

Automated bidding

Automated bidding is one of the two types of Google Ads bidding strategies. The other is manual bidding which is mentioned below. With automated bidding, the Google Ads system sets bids for you automatically based on your objectives and goals. So, the bids are set at auction time to bring the best clicks and conversions for your ads.

Maximise clicks

This bid strategy aims to get you as many clicks as possible for your budget. The Google Ads' machine learning system automatically sets bids to help your campaign get as many clicks as possible.

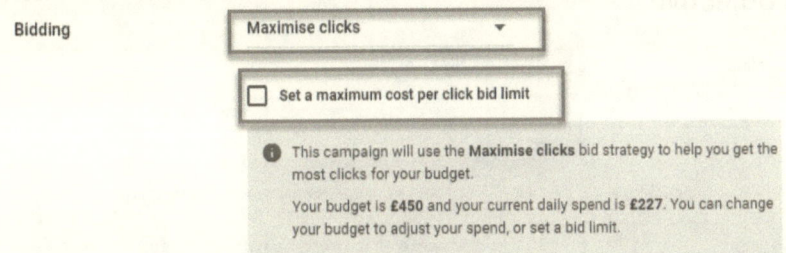

Setting a bid cap helps to control the maximum amount that you're willing to pay for each click. However, that can often limit the system from bidding effectively so you should test this and keep adjusting to see how it works for you.

You can use it as your bid strategy for one campaign or use it as a portfolio bid strategy and group multiple campaigns into a single strategy.

When to use

It's best to use maximise clicks when you've just created your campaign and launched it because you won't have any conversion data at this point. The system helps you see which of your assets are converting and then later you can change to a conversion-focused bid strategy.

Maximise conversions

Maximise conversions is an automated bidding strategy that focuses on getting you as many conversions as possible for your budget. It is one of the smart bidding strategies that focus on conversions and uses machine learning to achieve its objective.

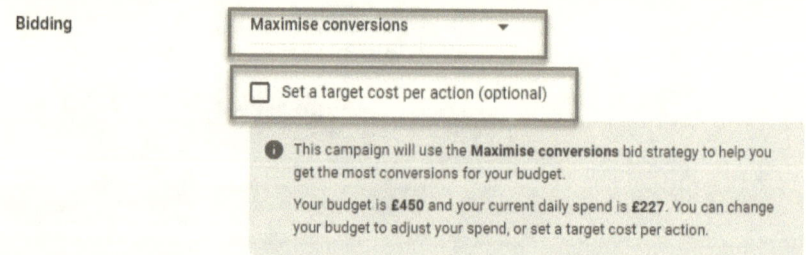

When to use

The best time to use this bid strategy is when you've been running your ads for some time and have some conversion history. So, if you've had at least 30 conversions in the past month in your search campaign, now may be the time to change to maximise conversions.

Target cost per action (CPA)

Target cost per action (CPA) is related to the maximise conversions bid strategy mentioned above, in your search campaigns. When you select maximise conversions, you have the option to set your target cost per acquisition.

For other campaign types, like a video campaign, this is a stand-alone bid strategy and is separate from maximise conversions.

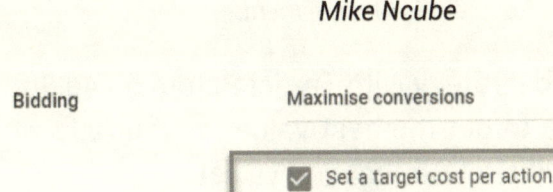

When to use

If you've been running ads for some weeks or months, and have been getting conversions, you're likely to see a recommended CPA based on your past average cost per conversion. You can use this recommended one or set one that is appropriate for your business. However, bear in mind that if you set the CPA too low, your ads may not appear when they are set to perform, and this will affect performance.

Maximise conversion value

Maximise Conversion Value is one of the smart bidding strategies that focuses on conversions. As one of the Google Ads automated bidding strategies, it sets bids automatically to help you get the most conversion value within your budget.

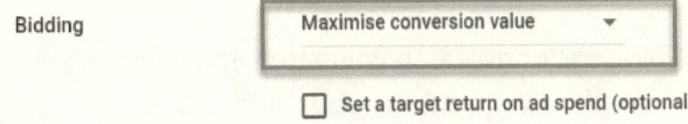

You can use this bid strategy with Target Return on Ad Spend and it will optimise to get the best value for your ads while aiming for the specific return that you've set.

When to use

If conversion value is as important or more important than just getting sale or lead conversions, then this bid strategy is for you. It will bid automatically and prioritise ads that will bring you the most value based on your goals.

Target return on ad spend

As mentioned above, target return on ad spend (tROAS) is a bid strategy that works with Maximise Conversion Value to help you achieve your objectives. It's an option that you can select as the screenshot below shows, and if you've been running your campaign for some time, you'll see a recommended tROAS.

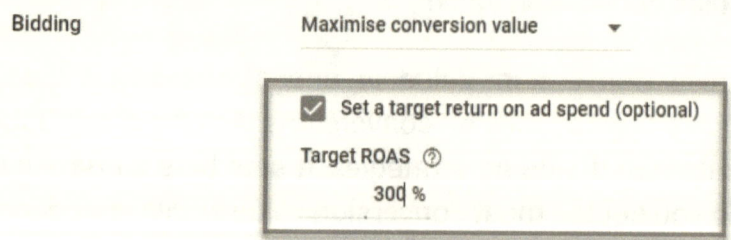

This is the average conversion value that you'd like to achieve for every pound you spend on your ads. So, you'll enter a percentage value like 500% if your goal is to get £5 in sales for every £1 you spend on your ads.

When to use

Use ROAS when you've been running your ads for some months and have achieved at least 50 conversions in the past month for your search campaign. Then, set your ROAS in line with the performance you've had and what you want to achieve. You can test various percentage returns but allow the system to run for at least two weeks after a change.

Target impression share

target impression share is an awareness-based bidding strategy. The aim is to get you as many impressions as possible and to make your ads more visible for your budget. So, it bids automatically and places your ads in one of the three locations that you choose: anywhere on the results page, top of the results page or absolute top of the results page.

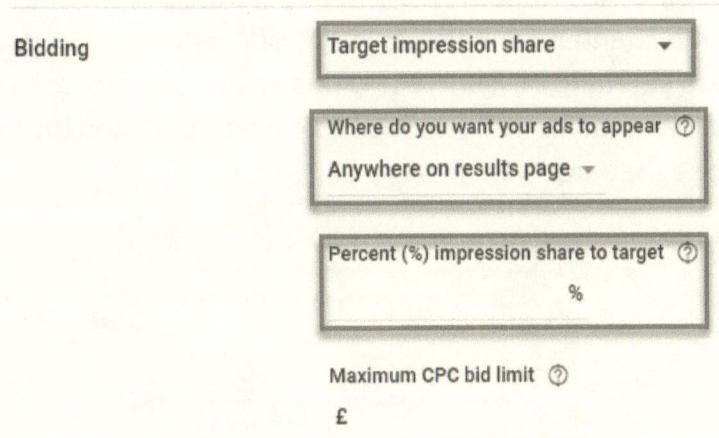

You must set a percentage impression share target that states how often you want your ads to appear in the search page area you choose. For example, you can set it to 50% if you want it to appear in that location half of the time.

When to use

This bid strategy can help you to be more competitive on the results page. For example, if you have some competitors you want to outrank, you can set it to appear in the 'absolute top of results page' for 100% of the time, or another percentage of the time you choose. It also helps you to be visible especially when your audiences are not seeing your ads as often and you are not spending up to your budget limit.

Enhanced CPC

Enhanced cost per click (eCPC) is slightly different from the other Google Ads automated bidding strategies in that it works with manual CPC to get more conversions. So, your core bid is set manually, and eCPC raises your maximum CPC bid for clicks that are likely to lead to conversions and lowers it for those that are least likely to convert.

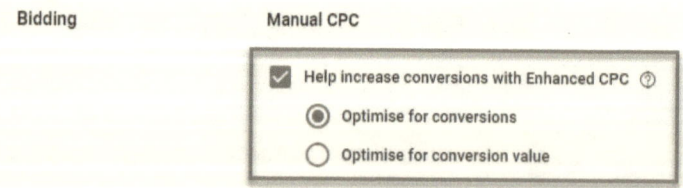

When to use

When you want to set bids manually and have more control but also want to leverage the power of automated bid strategy. This combination usually results in greater performance than just using manual bidding.

Manual bidding

With manual bidding you set your bids individually at the ad group or keyword levels. So, you'll set a maximum CPC bid limit to cap the amount you'll pay for each click.

Manual CPC

There is only one manual bid strategy, manual CPC, and it differs from the other bid strategies above that do auction-time bidding, and not ad group and keyword level bidding. So, it gives you more control over the maximum amount you want to pay for each click because you can set a maximum CPC.

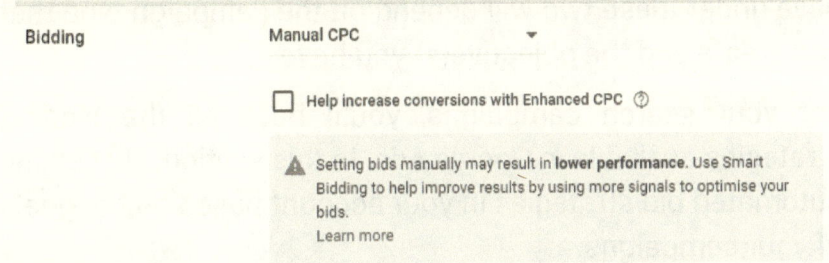

When to use

Use manual CPC when you want to have more control of your bidding, especially at the keyword level. This gives you greater control than automated bidding strategies, but it can also lead to inefficiencies and underperforming ads when not done correctly and/or monitored. So, it takes more time to manage and monitor.

Using Google Ads' automated bidding

Google Ads' automated bidding is a strategy that sets bids automatically for your ads based on the ad's likelihood to result in a click or conversion. There are at least four automated bidding strategies, and you'll use them at different times and based on your objectives.

Automated bidding takes the heavy lifting and guesswork out of setting bids. So, there is no need to set bids manually because the machine learning system sets bids for you automatically at auction time.

Automated bidding strategies learn as they go, using past bid performance to inform future bids.

In Google Ads, you can use automated bidding or manual bidding in your campaigns. The bidding strategies that you'll have under these two will depend on the campaign type that you create and the objective(s) you have.

For your search campaigns, you'll have all the bidding strategies available in Google Ads. In this section, I list all the automated bid strategies in your account based on the goals of your campaigns.

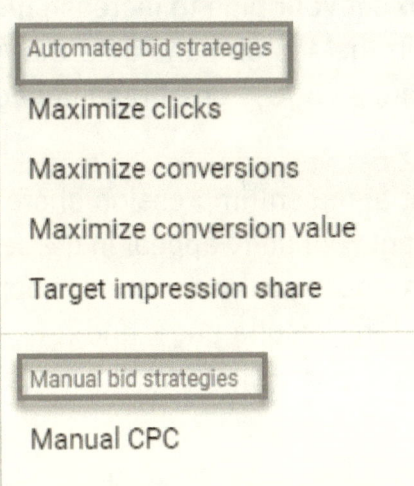

Awareness-based bidding strategies

Awareness-based bidding is a Google Ads automated bidding strategy that focuses on making your ads more visible. So, this helps you focus on specific locations, particularly higher ones to ensure that you are meeting a specific impression share threshold.

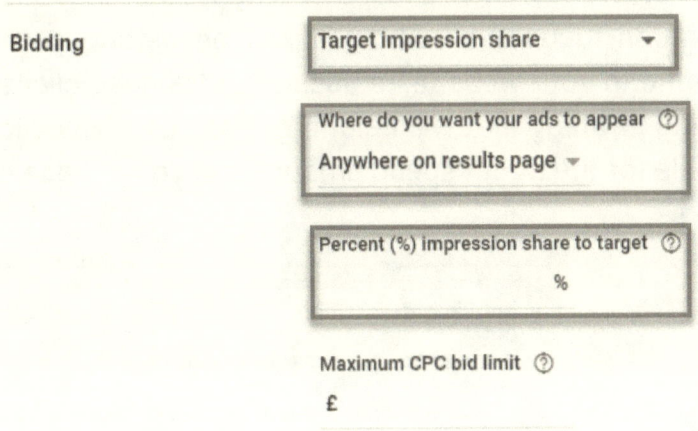

This helps you to set your bids to increase the chances your ads will appear in the search page area that you select, like 'anywhere on results page', 'top of results page' or 'absolute top of results page'.

You can then set a percent impression share target to state how often you want your ad to appear in the search page area you select. For example, you can choose to appear 50% of the time at the top of the results page, and it is also advised to set a maximum cost per click (CPC) bid limit.

When to use

Impression share target will also help you to outbid competitors. If you want to appear higher than all your competitors, you can set your ads to appear in the absolute top of results page, but make sure you set a maximum CPC limit because this can be very expensive if competitors are doing the same.

Consideration-focused bidding strategies

Consideration-focused bidding focuses on getting you as much traffic to your website as possible. Maximise clicks is the bidding strategy that will help to get you as many clicks as possible for the target spend amount that you choose.

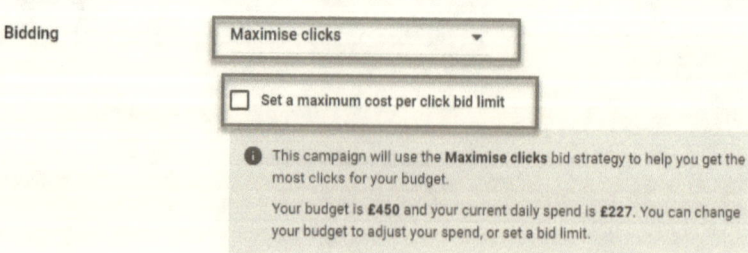

Your bids are set automatically at auction time by the machine learning system, and it positions your ads to get you as much traffic as possible for your budget.

You can also set a maximum CPC bid limit to cap how much you pay for each click. But this could limit the clicks you get on your ads.

When to use

As a consideration-focused automated bidding strategy, maximise clicks is the best strategy when you first launch your campaign. It helps you to see which of your searches are converting well and which are not and need blocking. Then, you can switch to a conversion-focused bid strategy when you have more data.

Conversion-focused bidding strategies

A conversion-focused automated bidding strategy has the greatest number of bidding strategies than the other types. These strategies include maximise conversions, target cost per acquisition (tCPA) and enhanced cost per click (eCPC).

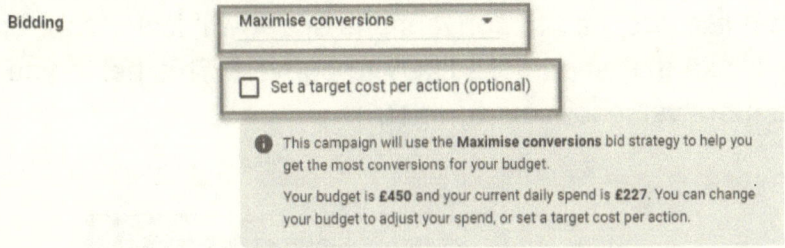

These strategies help if you're tracking post-click actions, are looking to value conversions equally, and to maximise the number of conversions your campaign is getting.

When to use

Change to one of these strategies later when you want to focus on conversions. For example, if you've now had at least 30 conversions per month and have an idea of how much you want to pay for each conversion, change to tCPA.

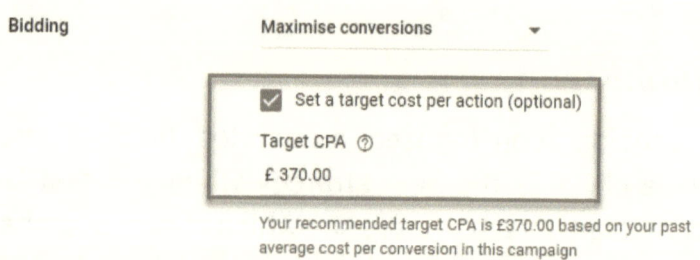

With maximise conversions, you'll be focusing on getting as many conversions as possible for your budget. The Google Ads machine learning system will have insights into which searches are performing best for your campaign and will adjust the bids to get as many conversions as possible.

And with eCPC, this helps you to set your core bid manually and then add a layer of real-time optimisation. This means your bids will be increased automatically for clicks that are most likely to lead to conversions and it will lower your bids for clicks that seem less likely to convert. This helps you to get more value for your budget.

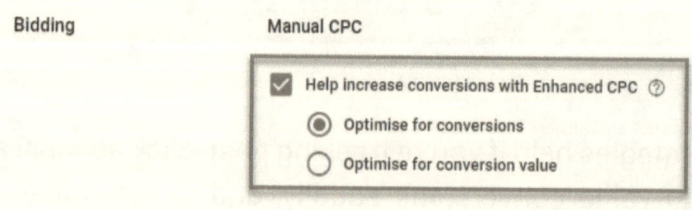

Revenue-focused bidding strategies

If you want to track the conversion value and have a search campaign that has had at least 50 conversions in the past 30 days, then revenue-focused bidding is the right fit for you.

With the target return on ad spend (tROAS) bid strategy, bids will be set automatically at auction time. This will help to get as much conversion value as possible at the tROAS that you set.

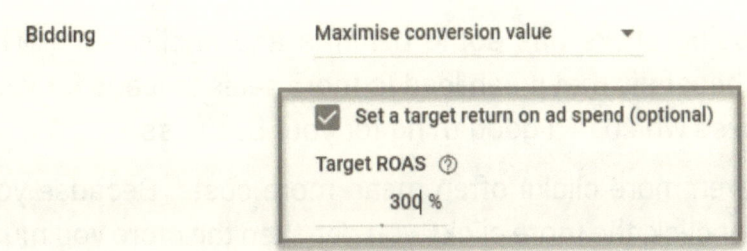

You will enter a value as a percentage. For example, if your goal is to get an average £3 in sales for every £1 you spend on ads, your tROAS would be 300%.

When to use

This is for you when you are sure of the return you want to receive for each £1 that you spend in your campaign. This will vary from campaign to campaign, but the system will try to achieve an average across them that meets your objective.

Which Google Ads bid strategy is right for your goal(s)?

Your choice of Google Ads bid strategy will depend on your objectives. So, if your objective is to increase clicks, impressions, conversions, conversion value or ad positions, you should ensure you pick the right bid strategy.

There are two bid types in Google Ads: automated and manual. There are at least eight bidding strategies to choose from under these two types.

So, to decide which one to use, check out the following objectives that I've provided below:

Increase Clicks

Increasing clicks has some benefits and implications. The main benefit is that it can lead to more sales or leads for your business which is a good thing for your business.

However, more clicks often mean more costs. Because you pay per click, the more clicks you get, then the more you must pay.

There are a few bid strategies that can help you get more clicks. The first is 'maximise clicks' which is specifically designed for this purpose. It will try to get you as many clicks as possible for your budget.

And it will set bids that will help you use as much of your Google Ads budget as possible and get you as many clicks as possible.

manual CPC bidding is another bid strategy that you can use to target click volume. Unlike maximise clicks which is an automated strategy, this is a manual strategy and lets you manage CPC bids yourself.

It allows you to set different bids for your ad groups, keywords, and placements, especially if you've found some of them more profitable than others. However, this can be time consuming if you have many keywords and placements in your campaigns.

Increase impressions and awareness

There are two main bid strategies to help you increase impressions and awareness. The first is target impression share, an automated bid strategy available for search campaigns.

This strategy helps to get your ads to the top position or absolute top position in the search results. Ads that rank at the top consistently have higher CTR and clicks overall, so you can get significantly more traffic.

Also, ads that are on the first page of the search results get a lot more impressions than those ranked on page two and beyond. In fact, over 70% of searchers don't look at the results on page two and beyond, so the more impressions you receive, the higher awareness your products or services will have. This helps to increase brand awareness.

Increase conversions and conversion value

You can use one of the four smart bidding strategies to increase conversions and conversion value. smart bidding strategies are a subset of automated bid strategies, and they focus on conversions.

They use Google Ads machine learning capabilities to set bids and increase conversions and their value. So, it's important that there's enough historic conversion data before using one of them.

Maximise conversions is a smart bidding strategy that you can use to increase conversions. It tries to get you as many conversions as possible for your budgets and it will set the bids to make that happen.

Target cost per acquisition (tCPA) is another strategy that you can use. You start by setting the average amount you'd like to pay for each conversion. It then starts working on an optimal bid for your ad every time that it's eligible to appear.

Just make sure you don't set a tCPA that's too low, which may lead you to miss clicks that could result in conversions.

Google Ads' bidding best practices

Google Ads' bidding is one of the important features in your campaign settings. So, it's important that you pick the best bid strategy to help increase clicks, impressions, sales, enquiries, or any other goal you have.

These are the latest Google Ads' bidding best practices to make your campaigns a success:

Start with an automated strategy

When you first create a Google Ads campaign, you're unlikely to know what bids to set. Of course, the keyword research tool can help with its 'suggested bid' feature and that can help you set a manual bid.

However, there are many factors that change constantly, like the competition, device used, locations and other variables that come into play during auction time. So, a suggested bid may not be very helpful.

With an automated bid strategy, you allow the system to set the bids. So, the Google Ads machine learning system sets bids based on your goals and it saves you a lot of time and effort.

But for some automated bid strategies, like smart bidding strategies which focus on conversions and conversion value, these will not be available when you first launch your campaigns.

You will have others like maximise clicks and target search page location. The former helps you to get as many clicks as possible for your Google Ads budget. It will set the bids automatically and tries to reach to get you as many clicks as your budget limit will allow.

Don't overbid

For some industries, being anywhere on the first page of Google will see an advertiser get sufficient traffic volumes to make Google Ads a success. Searchers will click most of the ads as they search for a product or service.

So, whether your ad is at the top or at the bottom of the organic results, you will still get many clicks. This is common with research heavy business sectors like ecommerce retail stores, so it's important not to overbid and pay over the top for your clicks, and that's especially true when you have a limited budget.

Your CTR will be high whether you're at the top or the bottom and being at the bottom could see you achieve a good cost per sale.

However, for other sectors like emergency services, it will be important to be one of the top three ads. This is because many searchers won't bother looking at the bottom ranked ads, they will go with one of the top ones.

Update low ranked keywords

If you're using a manual CPC bid strategy, some of your keywords will drop below the rankings on page one one. So, their rankings will be low and lead to a drop in impressions and clicks.

One solution is to use an automated bid strategy. It will take care of the bidding and help you reach your goals while saving you a lot of time.

CHAPTER 2

Budgets

One of the important things you will need to consider when looking to advertise online is what your Google advertising cost budget should be. This is especially true if you plan on advertising on Google and its partner websites and apps.

As effective as Google Ads is, it can only be truly effective for your business if you have a sufficient budget. Many businesses, including small ones, don't plan their campaigns effectively by doing some research and therefore allocate the wrong campaign budgets; it ends up either being too much or too little.

When done correctly, you'll quickly see which ads, keywords, campaigns, ad groups, etc., are working for you – and which ones aren't.

I've outlined some points that you should consider as you work on your budget for your Google advertising strategy. Hopefully, this should help you to better understand how to set a budget and update it to maximise the sales or leads for your business.

Advertising budget

The budget feature in Google Ads helps you set a daily limit on how much you want to spend. On some days, it will exceed your limit, especially when there is a high volume of searches, but you won't be charged more than your daily budget multiplied by the average number of days in a month (30.4 days).

Search campaign

For search ads, you can carry out keyword research to identify the keywords and search queries your ads should appear for. This is also very helpful in setting a budget that will determine your Google advertising cost. The Keyword Planner tool is available in your Google Ads account under 'Tools' and it's a free tool that you can use to carry out the research.

Shopping campaign

With shopping ads, your products appear in the search results when search queries match with product attributes. So, this is not based on keyword targeting like the search ads described above, but on the attributes you provide in your product feed. These attributes include product titles, descriptions, price, SKU, part numbers and so on.

Display campaign

One of the benefits of display ad campaigns is that the average cost per click is usually much lower than search ads. Your ads in the Google Display Network appear across a wide range of Google partners which include some Google properties like Gmail, YouTube and third-party websites, apps, and video sites. So, you can set a lower budget than you would, and that includes Display remarketing campaigns, too, which appear in the same placements. You will find your average Google advertising cost is much lower as you reach out to people that have been on your website and increase awareness for your brand and business.

Remarketing campaign

Remarketing, as mentioned above, helps to bring past visitors back to your website with the goal of converting them into customers. You can run remarketing ads via search, display and video campaigns on YouTube. Again, the Google advertising cost is quite affordable because there is, on average, less competition and therefore a lower cost per click. These visitors are not actively searching for your products or services when they see your ad. They are browsing a website or app and the ad helps them remember your business.

YouTube video campaign

A video campaign allows you to advertise on YouTube and its video partners. Using the Google Ads tools for video campaigns, you can run several ads on YouTube like in-stream and discovery ads. This helps you raise awareness for your brands, and you can promote your videos, website, products or services, and channels. Like display campaigns, these campaigns often have a lower CPC average, and you can start with a budget as low as $5 or £5 per day and then scale it up as performance improves.

Cost per click

The average cost per click for each visitor you get determines how many visitors you will get for your budget. You can limit the cost per click by setting a bid limit or allow the Google Ads machine learning system to set the bids, or you can run a manual CPC bidding strategy and control the bids at the keyword level to determine how much you will pay for each click.

It's important to note that you will not pay the actual bid amount you set, but an amount that allows you to clear the ad rank thresholds relative to the competitor immediately below you. This is often less than your bid – and sometimes significantly less. So, for example, if your bid is £1 and the next competitor has an 80p bid, you will pay 81p at auction time. This is known as your actual CPC and is determined by several factors like bids, ad rank, quality score and so on.

However, just bear in mind that your actual CPC will, at times, exceed your maximum CPC bid if for example you've enabled eCPC or if you've set a bid adjustment.

Knowing this helps you to set and adjust your budgets as you manage your campaigns and limit your Google advertising cost.

Business goals

Your business plan and goals should determine how much you will spend on your Google advertising costs. When you set a target for how many customers you need to acquire each month, for example, the keyword research tool will help to inform you on how many you are likely to get and what the conversion rate is likely to be for that.

You can then set a budget on the volume of traffic that you need and the average cost per click for that traffic. Google Ads has the Keyword Planner that you can use to carry out research and to run a forecast for the keywords you have selected.

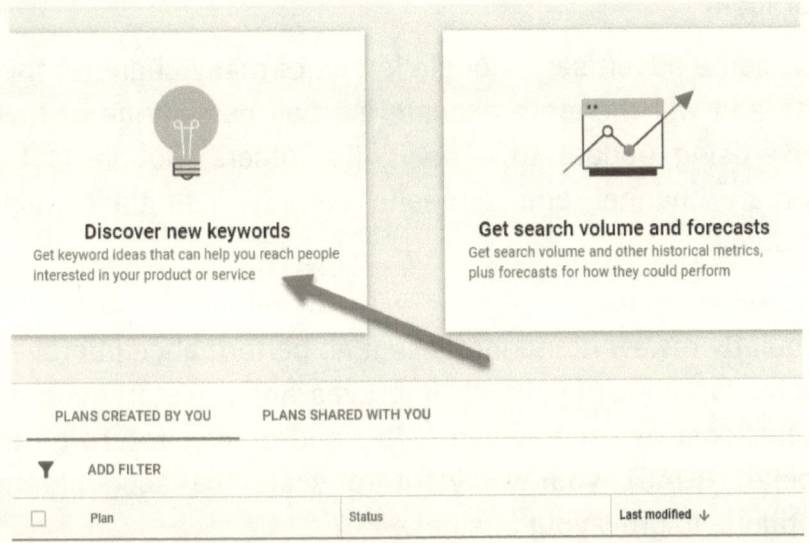

Type of business

The type of business you want to promote will also determine your Google advertising cost, too. Some industries are more competitive than others and some have very little competition on Google. Wherever you fall within that spectrum will help you decide what your advertising budget will be.

If it's a competitive sector, for example, insurance and loan industries where the cost per click can be easily over £20 per click, then a higher budget will be required.

Company size

The size of your company also has a bearing on your Google advertising cost. Large companies with millions in annual turnover generally have larger budgets compared to smaller ones. However, it depends on the actual digital strategy of the company.

For some advertisers, Google is one of many channels they use and will therefore allocate a small percentage of their advertising budget towards it. For others, Google is the primary channel, and it means everything to their online strategy.

Whatever budget you start with, it will be important to regularly review it and increase it as performance improves. As the targeting of your ads improves, and you start getting a better cost per acquisition (CPA) and greater return on ad spend (ROAS), you will want to scale the account and continue to grow your business.

Other factors to consider when setting your budget
Start with a test budget

A test budget can be low to test your ads, however, it shouldn't be so low that you end up taking a long time to assess the performance.

One factor to consider when setting a test budget is what the average cost per click is that you are aiming for. For example, if the average CPC is £1.30 for your keywords, then a monthly budget of £600 will bring in about 462 clicks.

On average, you should aim to drive 100 clicks per ad group to determine the performance. Of course, that is only helpful if you have created tightly themed ad groups with targeted ads and keywords.

So, with our example above of 462 clicks, you will have some ad groups that will have reached the 100 minimum clicks, and from this, you can assess the conversion rate.

If the industry average conversion rate is 3% and you've managed to achieve this, then you will have achieved about three sales for each ad group that has reached this minimum.

You can then adjust your budget according to the performance results you want to reach and continue to optimise your campaigns.

What are your goals for leads or sales?

Say your target is to get 200 leads each month through Google Ads, you'll need to work out what that will cost you. First, you need to work out your target cost per acquisition (tCPA) and the average conversion rate. If you've been running some campaigns, this will be easier to find.

However, if you're just starting out, then you should look at running some test campaigns first, and before you launch your ads, make sure you have set up conversion tracking.

With this data you can then change to a tCPA bid strategy. Your account will suggest a CPA to set based on its knowledge of the performance of your campaigns in the past, and it will then bid automatically and choose the right positions to help reach your target.

Check keyword volumes

Keywords are at the heart of Google Ads advertising. To set a good budget, you need to understand how big the search volumes are out there, and the way you find that out is by using a keyword research tool like the Google Keyword Planner tool.

As you can see in the screenshot below, this shows a forecast of what you're likely to spend:

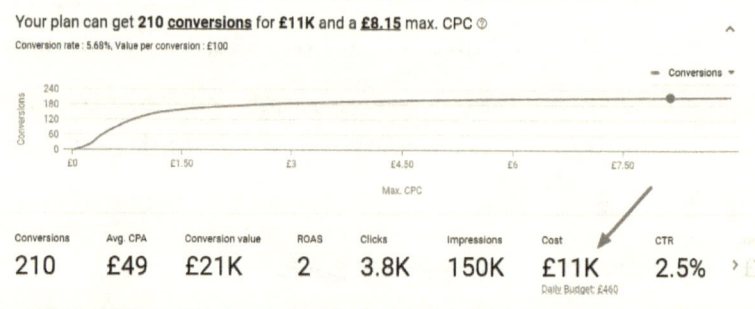

You can then adjust your bid in the tool to see what the average positions and CPC you will get. These, of course, are estimates but they will help to choose the budget that will help you reach your goals.

What is a suggested bid?

The Keyword Planner tool will also provide a suggested bid for many of your keywords. it will show you the level of competition for each: low, medium, or high.

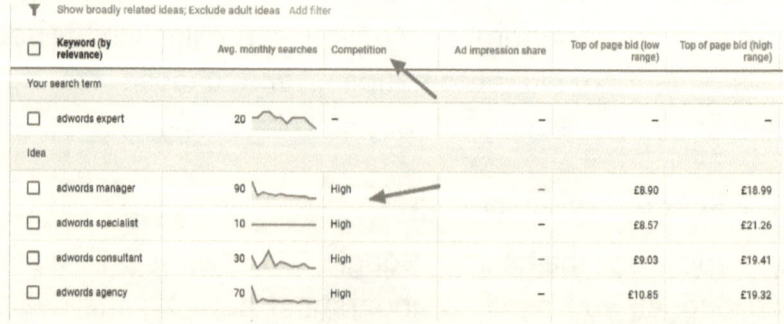

This is helpful if you will be using the manual CPC bid strategy. This is because when you first launch your campaign, you're unlikely to know what bids to set to achieve the best position and click results for your budget and goals.

It also helps with an automated bid strategy like maximise clicks because you can put a bid limit to prevent the system from bidding higher than you would want.

The suggested bids will then help you decide how much to set because you will know how competitive your keywords are.

Check competitors

One of the best tools to help you see how much your competitors are spending is Spyfu.com, and another is SE Ranking, which I've found very helpful when deciding on a PPC budget to set.

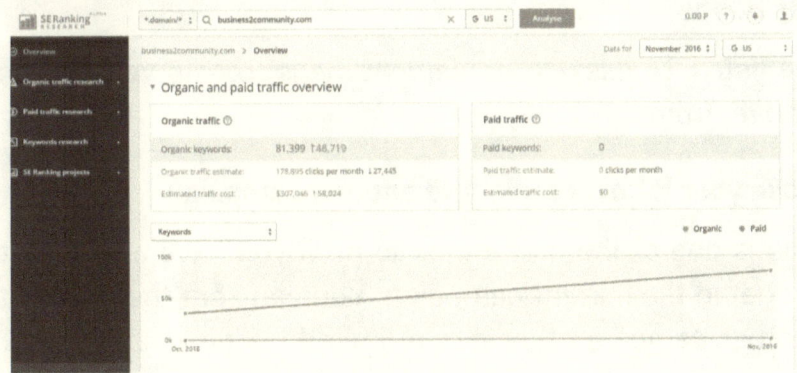

This tool also shows you:
- Keywords competitors are bidding on
- Which ads they are running for their keywords
- How much they are spending per keyword

- Keyword volumes for each keyword
- Whether their ads are ranked at the top or the bottom
- How much they are spending per month on average

This is powerful insight that will help you decide on a competitive budget.

14 savvy ways to spend any leftover in your Google Ads budget

If you've been running Google Ads campaigns for a while, you'll likely have come up with some creative ways to use your budget. This is important to achieve a good return on investment (ROI) for your ads.

However, you may have struggled at times to come up with ideas on how to use any leftover you may have in your Google Ads budget.

I've listed 14 easy-to-implement ideas to help you use any leftover from this budget:

Move your leftover budget to another campaign

This is one of the first things to do if you have any leftover budget in the current campaign. You can shift the budget to another campaign that has a limited budget and get more clicks and conversions through this campaign as well.

Create a shared budget

This is an easier way to use more of your budget in the current campaign. Instead of moving budgets manually, you can allow the Google Ads system to use more of the budget. You can do this by creating a shared budget in the 'Shared Library' section, deciding which campaigns can use the budget, and then assigning those campaigns to it to start using it.

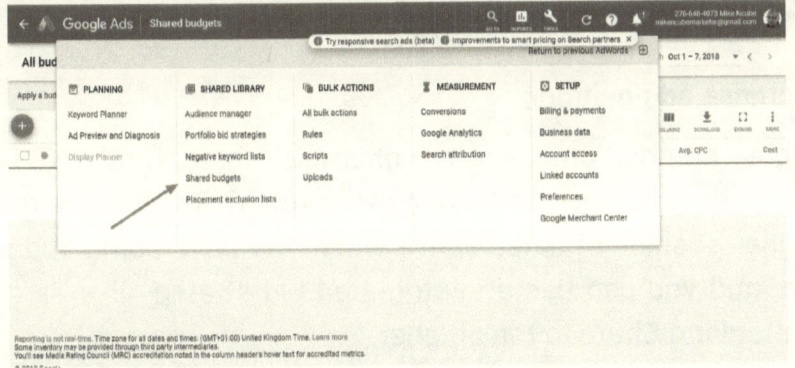

Add more keywords

One of the reasons you'll have leftover budget is because you're not targeting all searches. By adding more keywords, you'll target a wider range of searches which will increase traffic from more impressions and clicks. So, do some keyword research and look for relevant keywords to add in the campaign

Add broad match types

Adding broad match keywords of your already existing keywords will help you reach a wider audience. This will help you use more of your budget and get more clicks and conversions. This is one of the most effective ways to use your leftover budget.

Promote more products or services

If you have some leftover budget available, you could promote other products or services. So, you could create new Google Ads campaigns for them and do some keyword research to find relevant keywords and bid on them.

Increase ad positions

Higher ad positions lead to higher click through rates (CTR) which means more traffic and more spend. So, trying to gain higher positions makes sense when you have some budget left, and you can use an automated bid strategy like Target Outranking Share to rank higher.

Target other locations

A quick way to use your leftover Google Ads budget is to target additional locations. So, you can add other countries, cities, towns, or territories that could benefit from your products or services and are relevant to your business. You can add these to new or existing campaigns.

Update ad scheduling

If your ads are set to run on certain days and hours, then you should look to always run them 24/7. This will help you use up any leftover budget and increase the clicks and conversions for your PPC campaigns. When you make this change, Google Ads will immediately start running at the times when they were offline before.

Include search partners

If you're advertising on Google Search only, you can include search partners and advertise on other search engines. This includes YouTube and hundreds of other search partner sites which can drive many visitors to your site, and this is an effective way to use up any leftover budget.

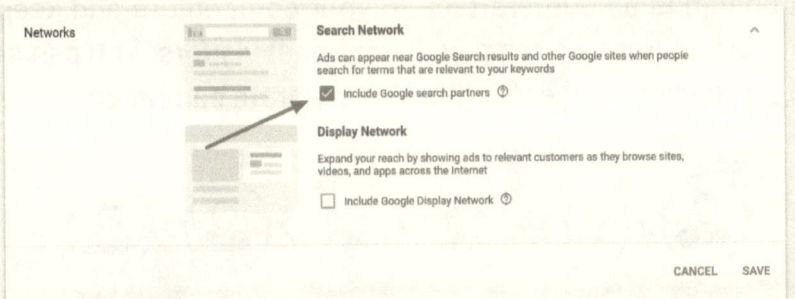

Target the Display Network

The Display Network has the potential to reach thousands of customers you wouldn't normally be able to reach with a Search Network campaign. You can raise awareness for your products or services by launching a display campaign and use your leftover Google Ads budget for this.

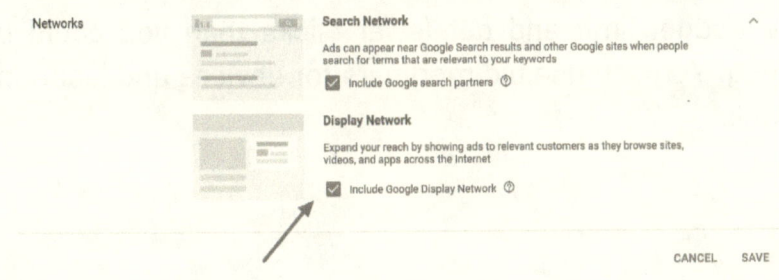

Set up a remarketing campaign

The purpose of remarketing is to bring people back to your website. Many visitors will leave and never return, and that's not necessarily because they're not interested in your products or services. Many things can distract them, including competitor offers, so setting up a remarketing campaign is a counterattack to your competitors and keeps your brand front-of-mind with your past visitors. You can set up a separate budget for this in a separate campaign.

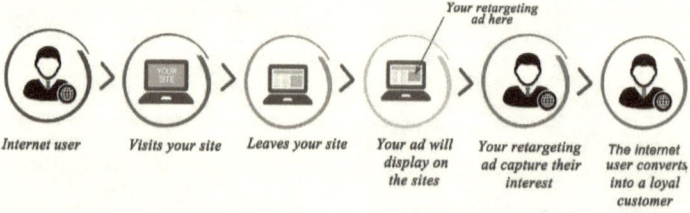

Use bid modifiers

Use bid modifiers to increase your bids and use up more of your budget. Using this will likely lead to higher ad positions and therefore lead to more clicks and a higher CTR. This is a quick method if you find that you consistently don't reach your budget limit and get fewer clicks than you could be getting. You can use bid modifiers for devices and locations as well.

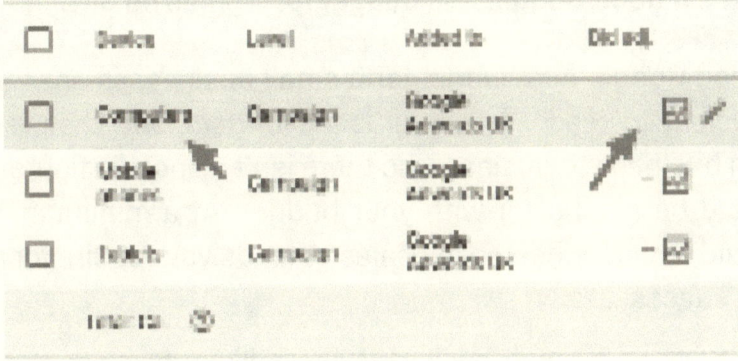

Target people outside your location

If you are targeting one country or city, for example, you could expand your reach to other locations by changing the advanced location options. This will lead to a significant increase in traffic and potentially more conversions, and if you regularly have leftover budget, you can solve that by targeting other locations that could benefit from your products or services.

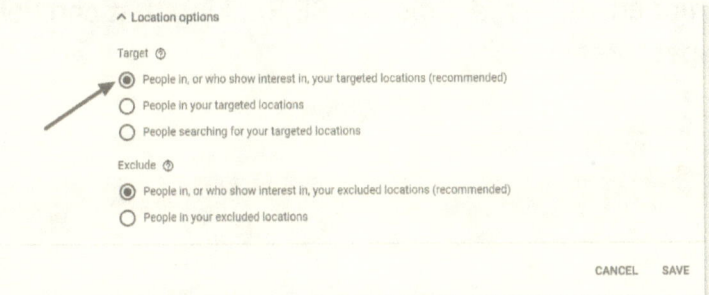

Target all device types

If you've limited device targeting to just a desktop or tablet or mobile, then you should target all devices to increase traffic and use more of the leftover budget.

What's a good Google Ads budget for a small business?

A good Google Ads budget for a small business is one that's sufficient to reach the advertiser's targets, and that varies from business to business, so there isn't a specific figure you should be aiming for with your budget. At a minimum, you should consider how many sales or leads you require for it to be a success.

However, as a small business you're likely to have a small starter budget that ranges from a few hundred to a few thousand each month.

Here are some factors to help you determine a good Google Ads budget for your small business:

Level of competition

Your competitors' budgets should be a factor when you're looking to assign a budget for your campaigns. It's not always easy to know what their budgets are. However, as mentioned, there are tools like SE Ranking that can help with competitor research.

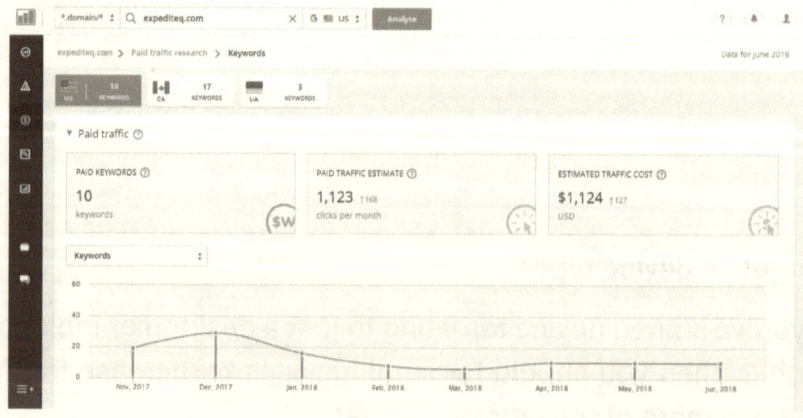

The competitor research will identify the keywords and ads in their campaigns. It will also show what positions they have for these ads and keywords and whether they're ranked at the top or bottom.

So, you can use some of these keywords as part of your keyword research, and you can create differentiated ads that are more relevant and can lead to high click through rates (CTRs).

Knowing what they are spending on average per month helps you to decide what budget to assign to your campaign.

Average CPC

Your keyword research will inform you whether competition is low, medium, or high for the keywords you want to use. It will also advise what bids to assign these keywords.

Your bid is the maximum amount you want to pay for each click. However, the actual CPC at auction time will be significantly less. You'll pay a penny more than the next ranked ad, so if your bid is £3 and the next ranked competitor has a £2.50 bid, you'll pay £2.51 per click.

Knowing what the average CPC is for your keywords helps you to determine how many clicks you'll get for your budget. If you find the click volume is too low to get any momentum for your campaign, then you should consider increasing the budget.

For example, if the average CPC for your keywords is £1 and you have a £500 budget per month, then you'll get at least 500 clicks on average. If this is too low, then you should either increase your budget or lower the CPC bid.

Impressions and click volumes

Keyword research is one of the first things you'll do to set up your Google Ads campaigns. This will inform you of the potential impressions and clicks, how many visitors you're likely to get, and will help to assign a budget. The Keyword Planner tool in Google Ads can help with this. It includes a keyword research tool and a forecasting tool to give you an idea of what you're likely to spend for the keywords you've shortlisted.

However, bear in mind that this is for 'exact match' searches of your keywords. So, this doesn't include the wide range of long tail searches that your ads can appear for. In fact, according to Google's own stats, about 15% of searches on their search engine are totally new to them and have never appeared before, so they won't come up in your keyword research.

Desired ad positions

Your ad rank is a big factor to what your budget spend will be. If you plan on achieving high ad positions, you should be aware that you'll pay higher CPCs and therefore spend more.

Ads that are in the top four positions spend considerably more than lower positioned ads. They have more exposure and therefore higher click through rates.

If these are the positions you want to secure, then you should budget for them. A few things you can do to achieve these positions is bidding higher, adding all applicable ad extensions, and creating relevant ads.

Conversion targets

If you know how many conversions you need daily, weekly, or monthly, it will be easier to set a Google Ads budget. As a small business, you should know how many sales or enquiries you need per month. This will help you to set the right budget.

It will also help you choose the right bid strategy, and you're able to use one of the smart bidding strategies such as target cost per acquisition (tCPA) and maximise conversions. These help you to focus on conversions and how much you're willing to spend per conversion so you can work on the budget.

Setting your Google Ads budget

Your Google Ads budget is set at the account or campaign level. The campaign level option is the most common and it's where you state the maximum amount you'd like to spend.

Setting this is straightforward. Go to the campaign you'd like to add or update a budget for and click 'Settings'. In the budget section, add the amount that you'd like to spend per day.

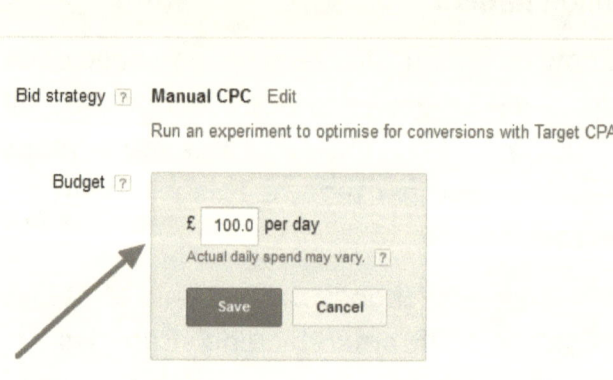

You can also set budgets at the account level. You do this in the shared library section and create a budget portfolio that you can assign to one or more campaigns. This is the main advantage of using an account level budget because it saves you a lot of time and helps you manage budgets easier.

To arrive at your daily Google Ads budget, you take your monthly budget and divide it by 30.4 (this is the average number of days in a month). So, if you're looking to spend £3,000 per month in your campaign, you'll divide that by 30.4 to arrive at a daily budget of £98.68.

This assumes that you want to advertise every day of the month. However, if you'd like to advertise on working days only, for example, then that could be about 22 days your ads will be active. So, your £3,000 monthly budget will equate to a daily budget of £136.

However, there's a difference between a budget and spend. Your budget is the maximum you want to put towards promoting your products or services on Google. The spend is the actual amount you're charged in your campaign.

It's possible to have a high budget but spend a very low amount. For example, if you have a monthly Google Ads budget of £2,000 but you only spend £800. This can happen if there aren't sufficient impressions and clicks to use up all the budget or if ads are ranked low and appear at the bottom of the page or on page two and beyond.

It's also possible to have a budget but overshoot it when traffic volumes are high. This will happen with your daily budget, but you'll not be charged more than your monthly Google Ads budget. Google allows this overshoot, to help advertisers get quality traffic when it's most important and ensure that you're always close to your maximum limit as some days are likely to be quieter.

Minimum Google Ads budget

Google has not set a minimum budget for advertisers to be able to promote their products or services on their search engine, so there's no such thing as a minimum Google Ads budget and you can set any budget that's affordable for your business.

This means you can spend as little or as much as you like. Some advertisers spend hundreds each month, some thousands and a few spend millions.

For new advertisers, the average Google Ads budget is £500 per month. This is usually a test budget to assess what works and what doesn't, and this is usually sufficient for most new advertisers, but that will depend on the competition. If competition is high with many advertisers going after the same keywords and positions, then the average cost per click

(CPC) will be high and so the budget will have to be higher, too.

For more established advertisers, higher monthly Google Ads budgets are common. Many advertisers spend thousands each month and this leads to many sales and conversions for their Google Ads campaigns.

Google Ad costs

The costs for Google Ads vary from business to business. There're many factors that go into these costs including competition levels, average CPC rates, ad positions and more.

Google Ads is a pay per click (PPC) advertising platform, so you only pay for clicks to your website and nothing more. Unlike other advertising platforms that charge for space and visibility, Google Ads only charges for visits to your website.

However, there're other charging formats like cost per thousand impressions (CPM) on display and view campaigns on YouTube, but PPC remains the core pricing format.

Your average cost per click (CPC), for example, will be determined at auction time. So, you're unlikely to know what that is until you run some test campaigns, but there are research tools in Google Ads that will help you forecast CPC rates for your keywords and what the likely spend will be.

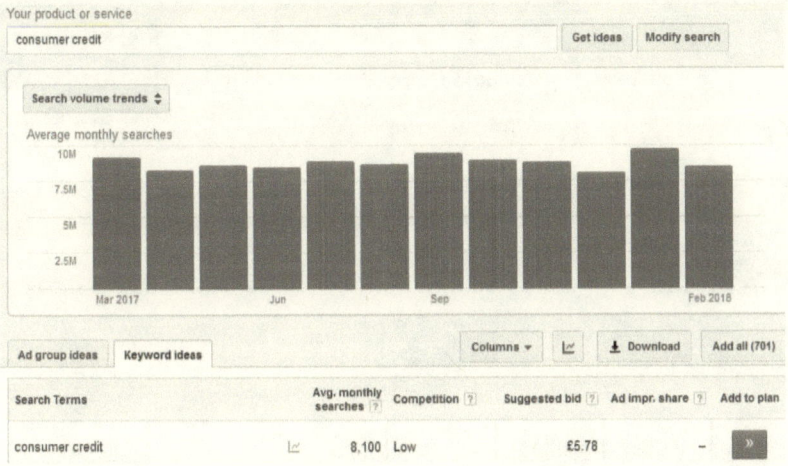

Controlling costs in Google Ads is important, of course. There's no point in spending a fortune and getting back little or no results. However, what's more important is the return on investment (ROI) your campaigns achieve.

One of the benefits of Google Ads advertising is that you can change and update your budget spend easily, and you can do that daily if necessary. If, for example, you've started with a daily budget of £50 and decide you want to reduce it to £40, then that can be done easily.

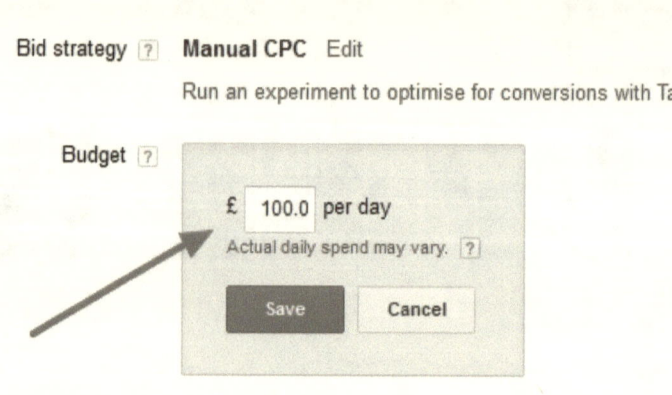

very method (advanced)

It's important to bear in mind that the average CPC rates vary from sector to sector. It's common to find rates as high as £15 for keywords in the insurance sector. For other sectors, CPC rates can be as low as 20p because of less auction time competition.

So, for these, starting with a low budget is fine. However, conversion rates can often be low for these less competitive sectors, and you may have to start with a higher budget to get a decent number of conversions.

Is Google Ads always expensive at the beginning?

The answer to that depends on several factors. Firstly, 'expensive' is a relative term and what could be expensive for one advertiser, could be a very small spend for another. This is true for competing advertisers in similar industries.

Also, you should consider the cost of Google Ads compared to other channels and what returns you get from each. Some channels like social media are 'cheap' but returns are sometimes much lower.

However, it's often true that the average cost per click (CPC) can be high at the beginning and can cost slightly more. This is usually because your keywords will have no quality scores, so you will have to bid higher for a higher ad rank.

One of the advantages of advertising through Google Ads is that you can start with a low/test budget. That budget can be as low as you want, and many advertisers start with budgets as low as £10 per day to assess possible returns.

Also, adjusting your Google Ads budget is easy and can be done at the campaign level. This allows you to limit your spend at the beginning and then scale as you achieve good return on investment (ROI).

You can also focus your budget on campaigns, ad groups, ads or keywords that are bringing you the best returns. The ability to control every feature of your campaign means you can turn off any poor performance campaigns and you can increase bids and budgets for the best performing ones.

Of course, there are some very competitive industries. Average CPCs of £7 and more are common as the image below shows:

Ad group	Status	Default Max CPC	Clicks	Impr.	CTR	Avg. CPC
Total - all ad groups			87	2,349	3.70%	£9.45
PPC Freelancer	Eligible	£0.01 (enhanced)	18	215	8.37%	£11.93
Adwords Specialist	Eligible	£0.01 (enhanced)	8	67	11.94%	£11.92
Adwords Expert	Eligible	£0.01 (enhanced)	20	393	5.09%	£11.65
PPC Specialist	Eligible	£0.01 (enhanced)	3	120	2.50%	£11.09

In such cases, you'll want to start with a higher budget to receive a reasonable amount of traffic. This will help you test your ads and keywords and learn quicker what is working or not.

So, is Google Ads expensive at the beginning? The answer is **no**, and that's because costs are easy to control with budget settings. Also, you're able to reduce spend on lower performing campaigns and focus on the ones with the best returns. It won't take long to figure out which campaigns those are as you will have that information within a few days or weeks.

CHAPTER 3

Click Through Rate (CTR)

Click through rate (CTR) is a measure of how effective your ads and keywords are at getting users to click through. It's calculated by dividing clicks by impressions:

$$CTR = \frac{Clicks}{Impressions}$$

A high Google Ads CTR is always desirable. You should take action to improve it for all your ads and keywords and look to maintain a CTR of 1% for your search campaigns.

To improve CTR, you need to know what affects it. I've included five key factors that contribute to your CTRs and recommendations on how to improve them:

Ad position

This is perhaps the most important factor to your CTRs. If ads are in the top positions, they'll consistently have higher CTRs than ads that rank at the bottom.

Even the most highly targeted ads that rank at the bottom will have low CTRs. So, it's important that positions for your ads are high and that you have a high ad rank if you want to achieve good CTRs.

An effective way to improve the click through rate is by using bid strategies like:

Manual bid strategy – increase bids manually for your keywords to rank higher.

Top of the first results page bid strategy – use this automated bid strategy to bid for higher ad positions.

Target outranking share bid strategy – use this strategy to outbid one of your competitors.

Ad relevance

Relevant ads attract more clicks. When users see that the ads are related to what they are looking for, they'll click through and that will impact CTR positively.

CTR impacts 'expected CTR', which is one of the factors to quality score performance and combined with 'Ad Relevance', another quality score factor, this can help you achieve good quality scores that are a good performance indicator for your account.

One effective way to make ads relevant is to add keywords in the ads. Users are more likely to click when they see their keyword in the ad. They'll ignore generic ads that don't speak to what they're looking for, so adding keywords in the ad will make your ads look relevant.

Bids

Bids are one of two factors for ad rank, and your ad rank determines the click through rate for your ads, with higher positioned ads getting a significantly better CTR. So, to achieve a higher position in the search results, you should bid higher to secure a higher position and achieve a good CTR.

Search terms

Each keyword will drive multiple searches to your ads. Some of these searches will be relevant and some won't. They'll each have their own CTRs, which you can see when you check the search terms report.

Benefits of improving CTRs

Improving your Google Ads click through rate (CTR) has several benefits, including:

1. **Increases traffic volumes** – when more people click your ads, you then have more visitors which has many benefits.
2. **Increases conversions** – with more visitors, you then get more sales and leads because you have more potential customers.
3. **Improves quality scores** – this is one of the three Quality Score factors, and when you improve Google Ads CTR, your scores increase too
4. **Higher ad rank** – your ads are rewarded with higher positions when they are relevant to searches.

Achieving a good CTR should be every advertiser's goal. You should continue to work on your targeting, ads, keywords, search terms, bids, positions and more to improve the click through rates.

Follow these tips to improve your Google Ads CTR:

Gain top positions

A top position on Google is a placement in one of the top four positions in the auction results. Ads that are at the top get significantly higher CTRs than those at the bottom below the organic results.

There are two main ways to gain top positions on Google: increase your bids and improve ad quality. Improving ad quality takes longer as you have to work on ad relevance and ensure that keywords are tightly themed in the ad groups and are related to the text ads.

Increasing bids is a lot quicker. You can increase bids manually if you're using a manual bid strategy or use an automated strategy to outrank competitors.

An effective bid strategy to outbid a competitor is Target Outranking Share. You can pick a competitor that ranks higher and appears at the top and use a Target Outranking Share strategy as the screen shot below shows:

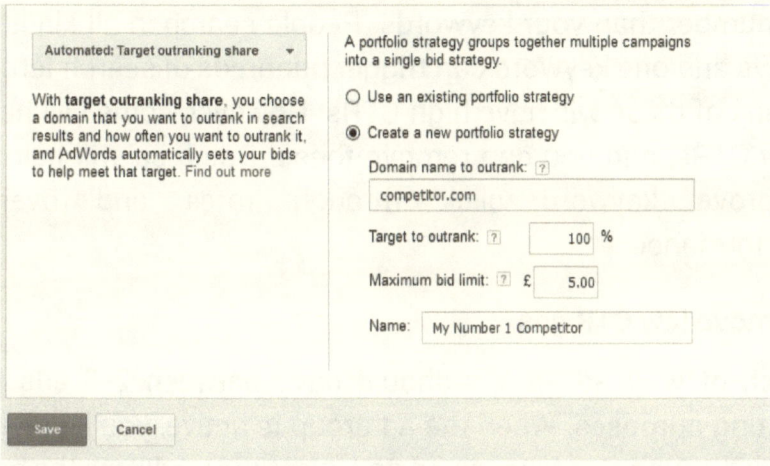

You can choose to outrank them all the time by adding 100% in the 'Target to outrank' section. Remember to put a maximum bid limit because this can get expensive quickly if they are doing the same.

Remove low CTR keywords

Check your campaigns for keywords with low CTRs. If your target is to have a minimum of 5% CTR, and some are as low as 1% or lower and with poor performance for conversions, too, then you should remove them.

Trying to improve these won't help. It will waste time which you could use to focus on better performing keywords.

Remove low CTR search terms

Check the search terms report to look for low performing searches. If they have low CTRs and conversions, then you can remove them by adding them as negative keywords.

It's not surprising to find search terms with CTRs as high as 100%. This is because search terms tend to be much higher in number than your keywords. People search in all kinds of ways and one keyword can trigger hundreds of search terms. Many of these will have high CTRs. However, some will have low CTRs, and you can remove these. Doing so will help to improve keyword click through rates and overall performance.

Remove low CTR ads

Each of your ad groups should have between 2-3 ads for testing purposes. When the ad group is active, you'll see the click through rate for each ad and over time you'll see the best and worst performing ones. You can replace low performing ads with better performing ones

Add ad extensions

Ad extensions give your ads more prominence in the search results. Adding many ad extensions helps to push your ads to the top as they become more relevant to searchers. Searchers are then more likely to click through, so try to add as many sitelinks, callout, structured snippet, call, price, and location extensions as you can.

Ad related to **adwords** ⓘ

Google **AdWords** 1 (866) 355 1410
www.google.com/**AdWords**
Be Found In More Online Searches Start Advertising With Google Today

AdWords Basics	Have Questions For Us?
An Intro to Advertising on Google.	Read Answers Here, or Ask Your Own.
Learn How **AdWords** Works.	Get Free Support from an Expert.
Real Success Stories	Set Your Own Budget
AdWords Users Share Their Stories.	Pay Only For Clicks on Your Ad.
See How Other Businesses Have Done.	Read About What **AdWords** Costs.

Include keywords in the text ad

Add the keyword in the ad. The best place to add it is in the headline, and Headline one in particular. This is the most prominent part of the ad and the clickable part that takes the visitor to your landing page.

People are more likely to click when they see their keyword in the ad. They'll perceive the ad to be relevant to what they need and that they'll find this on the landing page.

Of course, each ad group will have multiple keywords. In fact, each ad group should have at least five keywords, which makes it difficult to have every keyword included in the ad.

So, the solution is to use dynamic keyword insertion (DKI). This syntax replaces the default text that you add with the searchers keyword (bear in mind it's the keyword and not the search term that is included).

This is what the dynamic keyword insertion syntax looks like:

{KeyWord:Default Ad Text}

Read more about dynamic keyword insertion here.

Make ads relevant

The DKI syntax mentioned above is one way to make ads relevant. Another way is to add key benefits and a unique selling point to entice visitors to click. It also differentiates your ads from your competitors.

Many ads in the search results are drowning in a sea of sameness. Each one looks like the many others you can see on the page and aren't differentiated in any way, so searchers will click on any of the ones they see because there's nothing to differentiate them.

From now on, study what your competitors are promoting. Then look for ways on how to make your ads different by presenting your benefits and unique selling point.

If some of the search terms have high impressions and few clicks, then you should either look to remove them or improve their targeting. Doing so will help to improve your keyword CTR.

The keyword CTR is an average of all the search term CTRs for that keyword. If some of the search terms are underperforming and have low CTRs then you should remove them.

Ad extensions

Ad extensions give your ad more prominence in the search results. They make your ads stand out from your competitors' and encourage users to click through to your website.

Adding many targeted ad extensions for sitelinks, callouts, structured snippets, etc., improves ad quality, and this leads to a higher ad rank which results in higher click through rates.

So, you should add at up to 15 callout extensions, and as many sitelinks that are relevant. Also, add other extensions that are relevant for your business such as structured snippet extensions, price extensions, location extensions and call extensions.

What's a good CTR for a Google Ad?

A good click through rate (CTR) in Google Ads is only possible when ads are relevant to searches. If searchers find your ads related to what they're searching for, they'll click through.

However, there are many reasons why CTR may be low or high. A good CTR will vary from industry to industry and will depend on factors such as the position of the ads, campaign type, search intent, keyword type, device used and others.

So, it's not always easy to determine what a good CTR is, however, the following points should help to explain that better:

Below 1% CTR

CTRs below 1% are common for display and remarketing campaigns. This is because people are on websites that are part of the Google Display Network and aren't actively searching for your products or services, but they're checking out other content and are likely to ignore your image ads.

This is not a totally bad thing. Traffic volumes are usually higher for display campaigns, and it's expected that most people will not click your image ads. The people who click through are usually highly qualified and these are the ones you're interested in.

For search campaigns, CTRs below 1% aren't good. This shows that your ads are not targeted to the searchers, or they are appearing at the bottom of the search results, so aim to rank higher by improving quality scores and bidding higher for keywords. Keywords with high ad rank generally have higher CTRs. They also help to increase clicks and conversions and help you see what works or doesn't quickly.

Between 1-5% CTR

Achieving CTRs between 1-5% is a good target for a new campaign. It's a good place to start and, with time and additional optimisation, this should be improved.

This CTR is common for shopping campaigns and many search campaigns with targeted ads. One way to improve these CTRs is to check the search terms reports and remove any that aren't targeted and/or have low conversions.

Above 5% CTR

If you're a charity that uses the Google Ad Grant, you'll need to maintain an average CTR of 5% as a minimum for your account. This is a new requirement for all charities running campaigns on Google Ads.

Failure to maintain that means your account will be suspended. Google has taken this step because of advertisers abusing the free funding. The challenge with this is that you can't bid higher than £2, so your ads may not achieve the top positions that's usually required to have a high CTR.

The first step will be to remove all low CTR keywords and search terms, especially one-word keywords. Then do some keyword research to find new long tail keywords that are targeted and will help you maintain that target.

For all other advertisers, achieving 5% CTR is not a must, but is a good target to aim for. It ensures your ads are targeted and people have interest in what you have to offer.

You can achieve this by bidding for higher positions and appearing in the top three positions, and you can optimise ads that have low CTRs.

Above 10% CTR

CTRs above 10% are great and are a sign of highly targeted ads.

These are common for businesses that offer services and target a local audience; think of businesses like accountancy practices, local tradesmen, legal services, and others that offer one or a few services will have fewer searches to target. It's easy to find out what they're looking for.

20%+ CTR

Click through rates above 20% are common with brand searches. People searching for a product brand, service brand or personality brand are likely to click through because they know exactly what they're looking for.

Search Terms	Keyword	Match Type	Added/Excluded	Clicks ↓	Impr.	CTR
mike ncube	[mike ncube]	Exact	Added	12	24	50.00%
ppc freelancer	[PPC Freelancer]	Exact	Added	10	75	13.33%
google ad services	[google adwords services]	Exact (close variant)	None	5	99	5.05%

You'll see this if you bid on your own brand name as above. However, if you're already ranking highly for your own brand name and no one is bidding on it, then you should not bid on your brand name as this will be wasted spend. These searchers can easily click on your organic listing and still come through to your website.

CTRs above 20% are rare for general searches. There's usually a lot of competition and searchers have many advertisers to choose from. Also, your ads are unlikely to be highly targeted for general searches, so you'll get fewer clicks.

Why it's important to have a high CTR in Google Ads

A high CTR for Google Ads is always desirable. It's a measure of the effectiveness of your ads with your target audience and anything above 10% is often great.

However, this varies for different sectors and keywords. Brand searches usually have higher searches that can be over 50%, and generic searches will often have CTRs below 1%.

High CTRs are easier to achieve when ads are in the top positions. When your ads occupy one of the top four positions above the organic search results, you'll achieve high CTRs.

If on the other hand, you have a low average position, with your ads below the organic results, you'll have lower CTRs than competitors and therefore lower traffic volumes. However, higher CTRs sometimes lead to a high average cost per click (CPC) because you often must bid higher to occupy those positions.

Helps achieve good quality scores

Expected CTR is one of three factors that affect your keyword quality scores. It's a prediction of what the actual CTR will be based on factors such as past performance, user location, device used, search term used and others, so it's important that all ads are relevant to searches you're targeting. This helps to get high CTRs and therefore improves quality scores.

High quality scores lead to better performing campaigns. They're a sign that your ads and keywords are well optimised and will achieve your advertising goals. They also help to reduce your average cost per click and you achieve higher positions for less cost.

Increases website traffic

A high CTR means more traffic because many people who see your ads click through to your website. If you get many impressions but a low click through rate, then you'll have few visitors.

There are many ways to increase CTR including:

- Adding keywords in text ads
- Using dynamic keyword insertion in text ads
- Bidding higher to increase ad position
- Removing search terms with low CTRs

Improves conversions

A higher CTR means more clicks and usually more conversions. The more people you get to your website the more likely you're to get more sales or leads. It's a numbers game.

Of course, this traffic should be targeted at people who're likely to be part of your target market. Usually, if the CTR is good, conversions also tend to be good as visitors are highly qualified. People who see your ad and click through will have found your ad relevant to their needs, so you are likely to see more conversions.

Achieves higher rankings

If your ads have high CTRs, they're generally perceived as relevant, so they get higher ad quality scores and are pushed up the rankings for less cost. It's a win-win situation for your campaigns and this increase in positions leads to higher CTRs. It therefore becomes easier to reach CTRs of over 10% for your campaigns.

What is an average CTR in Google Ads?

The average click through rate (CTR) varies for each business and from industry to industry too. It also varies for the type of Google Ads campaign that you are running.

Display campaigns, for example, usually have a CTR below 1%, and that's mainly because for display ads, people are not actively searching for products or services but are browsing third party websites that are part of the Google Display Network (GDN). So, any banners and text ads on a page are usually ignored. In fact, it's common to find CTRs as low as 0.05% in the GDN but still have a high conversion rate.

Search campaign CTR

For search campaigns, the CTR is almost always higher and will be above 1% because you are targeting people that are looking for your products or services.

However, CTRs below 1% are common for search campaigns, and this is often true for ecommerce searches. For example, people looking for shoes have a wide range of options to choose from and there is a wide variety of keywords. So, a high volume of searches and low click through rate are common. However, conversion rates may still be good which is what is more important.

For brand name searches, CTRs of 20% and higher are common especially for less competitive brand names. Bidding on your brand name or competitors brand name will usually result in a high CTR. The search volumes may be low, but performance for metrics like conversions and CTRs will usually be high.

Search term CTR vs keyword CTR

There's a difference between keyword CTR and search term CTR. In your search terms report, it's normal to see search terms with CTRs as high as 100%, but you will also find search terms with very high impressions but low CTRs. These are search terms that are usually not targeted because of the keywords and match types you have.

Remember, there's a difference between a keyword and a search term. A keyword is what you put in your campaign. A search term is what people use to find your ad on Google, and that is controlled by the keyword and is regulated by the match type you've used.

Overall, there's an acceptable average CTR across sectors and industries and from my experience, a service-based business should aim for at least 5%. Anything below that means the ads are not as targeted as they should be to the search terms. expected CTR is an important metric and is one of the three factors behind quality scores with the other two being landing page experience and ad relevance.

Working on each of these will help boost your quality scores and improve the overall performance of your campaigns.

CHAPTER 4

Conversion Tracking

PPC conversion tracking is a way to track actions on your website from your pay per click traffic. These actions include:

- Purchases on a website
- Enquiries on the contact form
- Submission on a booking form
- Calls from the website
- Calls from the ads
- White paper downloads

These are the popular ones and there are many more that you can setup.

Conversion tracking is available in Google Ads and it's a free tool that shows what happens when people interact with your ad. These interactions include purchasing, downloading, sending an enquiry, makes a call and others.

There are several reasons why you should setup PPC conversion tracking including:

- You get to see which ads, keywords, ad groups and campaigns are effective at driving valuable customer actions.

- It helps you understand your return on investment (ROI) and make informed decisions about how much you spend on your PPC campaigns.

- It allows you to use smart bidding strategies such as tROAS and eCPC. These automatically optimise your campaigns according to your business objectives. Without PPC conversion tracking, you'll only be able to use manual bidding and standard automated bidding strategies like maximise clicks.

- Get information on how many of your customers are interacting with your ads on one device and convert on another. You can see cross-device data by adding a column for 'All Conversions' in the reporting column.

Setting up PPC conversion tracking is straightforward, and you start by adding the tag or code snippet to your website or app. When a visitor clicks your ad and reaches your site, a temporary cookie is placed on their computer or mobile device.

When they complete an action like making a purchase, the Google Ads system recognises the cookie, and a conversion is recorded.

However, there are some types of conversion tracking that don't require a tag. These include tracking phone calls from your extensions or call only ads. You can use Google Forwarding numbers to track when calls come from your ads.

Also, you can track app downloads and in-app purchases from Google Play, and they will be automatically recorded without having to add tracking.

Why Google Ads conversion tracking is not working

Google Ads conversion tracking is one of the most important features in your account. As part of the setup of your campaigns, you should have a list of conversion actions that you want to track. These can include:

- Tracking online purchases
- Tracking offline purchases
- Tracking downloads
- Tracking newsletter signups
- Tracking leads on the contact form
- And many others

Failing to set it up correctly will affect the performance of your Google Ads campaigns and you're likely to waste a lot of money if it's not done right.

There are several reasons why your conversion tracking isn't working, and I've listed some of the main ones here to help you fix your tracking:

Conversion tracking not set up

If you cannot see any conversion data, then it's possible that it hasn't been setup. If your reports show zero figures for the following metrics, then it may have not been set up:

- Conversion
- Cost per conversion
- Conversion rate

Tracking code not installed

One of the main reasons why Google Ads conversion tracking isn't working is because the code hasn't been installed. Setting it up in Google Ads is only half the job. You also need to add the tracking code on the 'success' or 'Thank you' page.

It's advisable to add the tracking code as soon as you setup conversion tracking. That way you're unlikely to forget.

Also, you can check the source code of the tracking page to see if it has been added successfully. Check between the head tag of the page, which is where it should be added.

In WordPress, there are plugins that help you easily add tracking code. Check that they are compatible with your version of WordPress and check the reviews to assess how good they are before downloading.

Installed in the wrong place

If you install the tracking code in the wrong place, you won't have any conversion data. If the code hasn't been added between the head tag in your source code, then it's unlikely to be triggered when people complete a conversion action on your website.

Conversions not imported

If you've set up goals but have not imported them into Google Ads, then you won't have any conversion tracking.

When your Google Ads and Analytics accounts are linked, you can import goals into Google Ads and set up conversion tracking. This is a straightforward process that allows you to see how your campaigns are performing.

How to setup offline conversion tracking in Google Ads

Sometimes sales take place in the offline world such as in your shop or office and it can be difficult to know where they came from. So, by importing these sales into Google Ads you can measure what happens offline to get an overall picture of how your sales and ads are performing. This is after your ad results in a click or call to your business.

There are many benefits to importing offline conversion actions:

- It gives you a comprehensive view of which of your keywords and targeting drive the most cost-effective conversions. This can help you optimise your campaigns more effectively.
- Removes ads and keywords that aren't working for your campaign and are bringing in few offline conversions. This improves your return on investment.
- Tracks information about your calls such as call type and value and it ties this to the specific ad and keyword that drove it.

- Distinguishes between sales calls and support calls and learns the value of each of them.

How it works

There are two types of offline conversion tracking, and each works a little differently depending on whether you're tracking conversions that begin with a click or call from an ad.

Conversions from clicks

Google Ads provides you with a unique ID called a 'GLCID' for every click on your ads. To track offline conversions, you'll save the GLCID along with lead information you collect from the visitor who clicked your ad.

When that visitor converts by signing a contract in the offline world, for example, you give the GLCID back to Google Ads along with a few other details. Then this conversion is recorded along with other conversion tracking data such as the type of conversion and when it happened.

Conversions from calls

Importing calls requires Google Forwarding Numbers which are available in certain countries. This conversion tracking tracks calls that are the result of taps on mobile ads as well as calls that come through the website after a visitor clicks a desktop ad.

Importing call conversions into Google Ads helps you know which of your ads and keywords result in the most sales calls for your business.

How to set up Google Ads conversion tracking

It's important to set up Google Ads conversion tracking to be able to see how your ads, keywords, ad groups and campaigns are performing. Without tracking, you'll struggle to optimise your campaigns effectively.

The steps to set up conversion tracking are easy to follow, and within a few minutes, you can have it completed. You can do it all within Google Ads and then add the tracking code on your website or set up goals in Analytics and import them into Google Ads. These are the steps:

Link Google Ads & Analytics

First make sure Google Ads and Analytics are linked. You will need to create the goals in Analytics before they are imported into your Google Ads account, so it is important to do this step first.

Import goals into Google Ads

Now, you can import the goals into Google Ads and set up conversion tracking. Go to the tools section in Google Ads and then click on Google Analytics. You'll see the goals that are available to import.

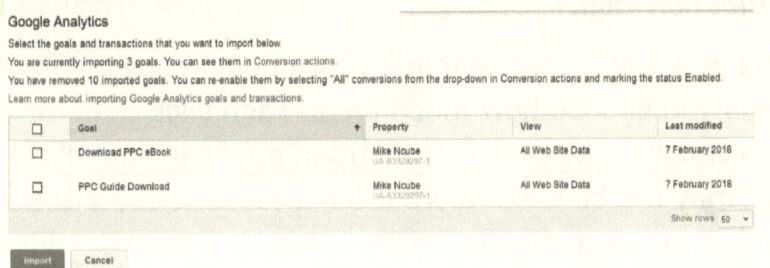

Select them one by one or all at the same time and then click import. It would probably be best to select them one at a time, especially if they are different conversion types.

Update settings

Next, update the following settings:

Category

What category does the goal fall under? Is it a purchase, a signup, a lead or just a view of a page? This is why it's important to import the goals one at a time if they fall under different categories.

Value

Next decide what the value of each conversion is to you. If you've set a value in Google Analytics you can choose to manage this over there and just import it too.

Conversion window

Choose how long after a click you'd like to track conversions. The default setting is 30 days, but you can change this to whatever you like based on your knowledge of your industry.

Attribution model

This is a feature for search and shopping conversions and helps you choose how much credit each click gets for your conversions. The default attribution model is 'last click' but that may not be ideal for your business. Use the attribution modelling tool to compare different models side-by-side.

Update columns

Finally, update the columns in your data reports. This helps you to quickly see how well your ads, keywords, ad groups and campaigns are performing for conversions. The three main conversion metrics to add are:

- Conversions
- Cost per conversion
- Conversion rate

Cost	Avg. Pos.	Conversions ↓	Phone calls	Cost / conv.	Conv. rate
£21,703.22	3.3	145.00	13	£149.56	4.78%
£47.59	1.5	16.00	0	£2.97	6.87%
£30.32	1.0	9.00	2	£3.37	9.00%

The differences between Google Ads and Analytics conversion tracking

You can setup conversion tracking in Google Ads or Google Analytics. Analytics conversion tracking is known as goal tracking and the setup process differs from the Google Ads setup.

However, before we look at some of the differences, let us look first at some similarities:

- You get to see how your ads, keywords, ad groups and campaigns are performing with both.
- Both have reporting tools that you can see in your accounts.
- They are free tools.

So, now we'll look at the differences between Google Ads and Analytics conversion tracking:

Set up templates

Analytics conversion tracking provides several customised templates to help you setup your goal conversions. The templates available depend on the nature of your business and the details you provided when you signed up to Analytics.

The templates fall under categories such as acquisition, engagement, enquiry, and revenue.

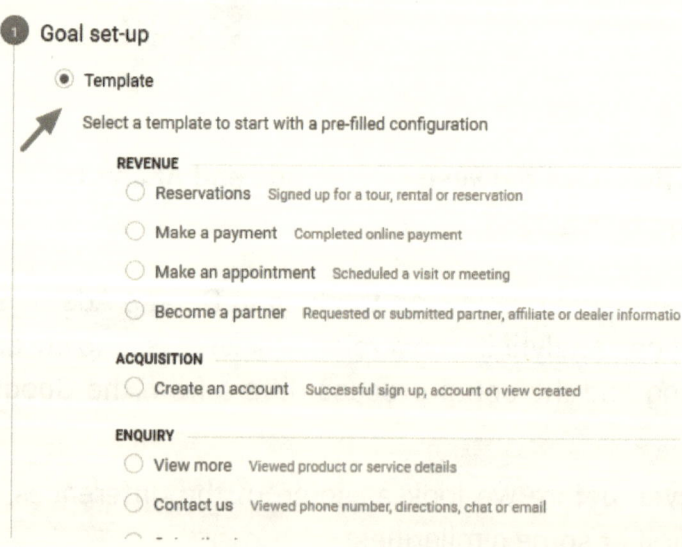

Google Ads conversion tracking doesn't provide any templates. All you get are five category options which are based on the type of action that you'd like to track.

Tracking code setup

One of the advantages of setting up Analytics goal tracking is that you don't have to add an additional code for each new goal. You can create up to 20 goals in Analytics and you won't have to add a code to your website.

With Google Ads conversion tracking on the other hand, you'll have to add a tracking code to your site for each conversion you set up.

This can be time consuming and is prone to errors. It's possible that the code can be entered incorrectly at times. It also slows down your website, especially if you've uploaded many tracking codes.

With Google Analytics, you only add the JavaScript tracking code once when you first setup the Analytics account and you then set up the goals in the admin section without adding more code.

Reporting

One of the disadvantages of Google Ads conversion tracking is that this information will not be available in your Analytics reports. To have conversion data in your Analytics reports, you'll need to set up goal or ecommerce tracking in Analytics.

Reporting in Google Ads is not as advanced as reporting in Analytics, so if you want more in-depth reporting that includes conversions, then you need to set this up in Analytics.

Multi-channel funnels

One of the major benefits of Analytics goal tracking over Google Ads Conversion tracking is the multi-channel reports. These reports reveal how different channels contribute to the goal conversions that take place on your website.

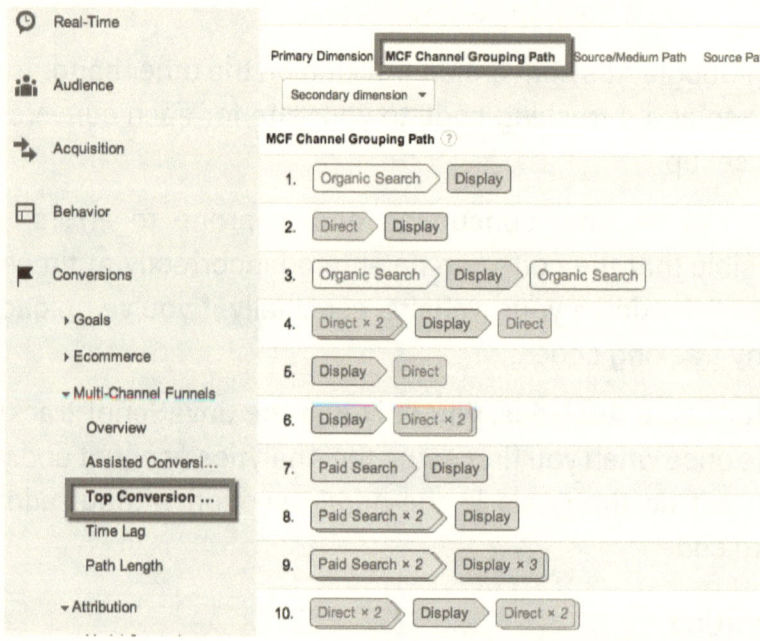

This reporting requires goals and ecommerce tracking to be enabled for the Google Analytics view. Unfortunately, you don't get such detailed reporting if you have only set up the Google Ads conversion tracking.

Multi-channel funnels help you to see which are your most important channels. Some channels may be great at introducing people to your business but not in the final stages of conversion, so you'll still want to utilise these channels and use them to raise awareness for your products or services.

CHAPTER 5

Cost Per Click (CPC)

CPC or cost per click is a marketing model that charges you only for performance, like when people click your text ads or phone number in the ad results. So, you set a maximum cost per click bid or 'max CPC', which is the highest amount that you're willing to pay for each click.

However, this is for when you're using manual bidding when you set bids yourself. With automated bidding on the other hand, the system sets bids automatically based on your goals like impressions, clicks and conversions.

Google Ads is the leading CPC marketing platform which displays ads on the Google search engine and its partner websites and apps. It's also known as pay per click (PPC) and is a performance-based platform that gives you a lot of control over your advertising costs and strategy.

Here are some key features of CPC marketing in Google Ads that help you run effective campaigns.

Campaign type

There are different campaign types that you can run as part of your CPC marketing. On the Google Ads platform, you can run PPC campaigns in search, display, shopping, video, local, smart, performance max, discover and app formats.

Each of these campaign types has its purpose and helps you achieve specific goals for your business. For example, search is the primary CPC campaign type in Google Ads, and you use keywords to target people who are searching for your products or services on Google and other partner search engines. So, as people search and click your ads, you're charged for each click.

For shopping campaigns, you provide a product feed to the Google Merchant Centre and link it to Google Ads. Then, you create a shopping campaign in your Google Ads account so your product listings can appear in the search results above the text ads and on the shopping tab. Like other campaigns, you're charged every time someone clicks your ads.

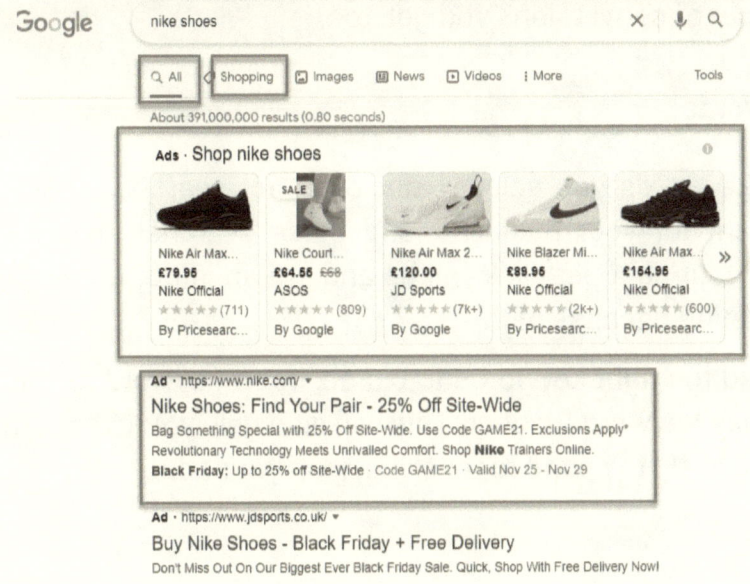

Text ads

Text ads are the primary ad type in Google Ads. There are other ad types like image ads, responsive display ads, dynamic search ads, call only ads and product listing ads. Your text ads are what people see when they search for your products or services on Google, and they are an important part of CPC marketing.

When people search on Google and see your ads, they can click through to your website to find out more. You are only charged when your ads are clicked. If they search but do not click the ad, you will not be charged, so the benefit is that you only pay for traffic that is likely to convert. The budget you set determines how many clicks you get and that affects the number of conversions you get, too.

Keywords

The keywords you select help to attract searches that are relevant for your business, and these searches determine what your cost per click will be and are an important of CPC marketing because of this.

To find the right keywords to bid on, use a keyword research tool like Keyword Planner. This will also help you to see what you're likely to spend for each click on your ads.

Start with phrase and exact match type keywords to control the searches that you get to your ads. This helps you to get a better indication of what your average CPC will be.

Bid strategy

Your bid strategy is a very important part of your CPC marketing. It's one of the main factors that determine what your cost per click will be for each visit to your website.

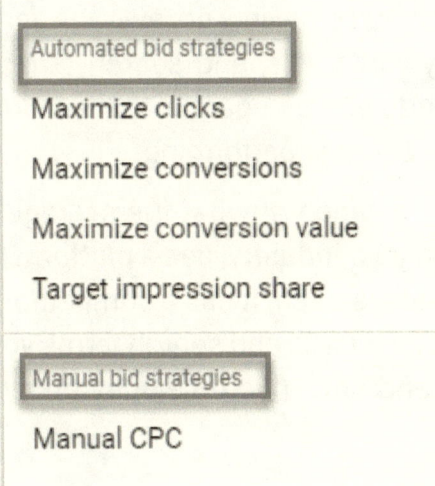

There are different bidding strategies to pick from, including automated and manual options as the screenshot above shows. The bid strategy you decide to start with depends on your goals. Some help you focus on impressions, some on clicks and some on conversions and conversion value.

You can use each strategy at different times. The maximise clicks bid strategy, for example, focuses on getting you as many clicks as possible for your budget. Later, you can change to a conversions-focused bid strategy when you have a lot more data.

The manual CPC bid strategy gives you more control over your bids, so you can set a maximum amount to pay for each click.

What is the average CPC in Google Ads?

The average cost per click (CPC) in Google Ads helps you to see how much you're paying on average for your account, campaigns, keywords, ads, and search terms. You can see this in your reports and compare with the industry average to see how your account is performing.

To get a good indication of what the average CPC is among competitors and your industry, use a platform like SE Ranking to carry out some research. It has a competitor tool that helps you to see what keywords and search terms your competitors are bidding on and how much they pay on average for each click.

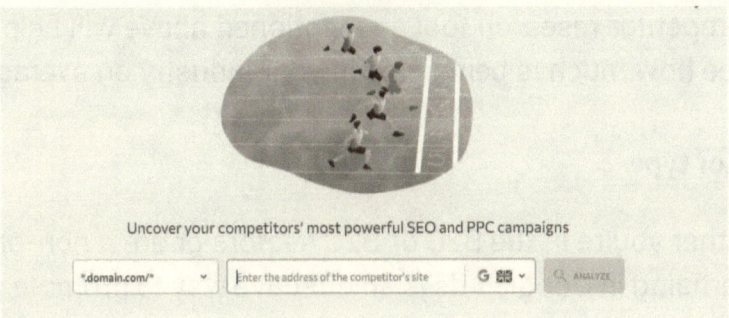

This helps you to select the keywords to bid on and the budget amount that you'll set.

I've included some guidance below on what the average CPC is for different industries, sectors, keywords, and campaign types, and hopefully, this should help you set the right budgets and manage your campaigns effectively.

Industry type

The average cost per click (CPC) in Google Ads varies from industry to industry. Some industries and businesses experience very high CPCs while some pay pennies to drive clicks and conversions to their websites and businesses.

The finance industries usually have higher costs due to the competitive nature of this space. There are many advertisers vying for the same space and to get noticed. For example, keywords related to 'bridging loans' can average about £15 per click for search campaigns.

On the other hand, online retailers of custom products like gifts or candles could pay as little as 6p per click for shopping ads. This is because there is less competition, especially for custom products that do not have direct competitors. Using a competitor research tool as mentioned above will help you to see how much is being paid in your industry on average.

Sector type

Whether you're in the B2B or B2C sectors or are a non-profit, advertising in Google Ads is an effective way to promote your products or services. As people search you can target them with ads and keywords that relate to your products or services.

B2B businesses usually have fewer keyword searches than B2C and so the average CPCs are usually higher because of competition chasing the same keywords. For example, local accountants targeting small to medium businesses will often pay over £3 per click to drive visitors.

But for B2C the range of keywords and search terms is usually much wider especially for ecommerce sites and retailers and average CPCs can be below 50p per click. they can be even much lower for Shopping ads where there is usually less competition than Search ads.

But this will differ widely at times and from business to business. So, carrying out some keyword research and competitor research will help you understand what you're likely to pay.

Campaign type

The average CPC in Google Ads also varies from one campaign type to another. There are several campaign types in your account, and these include search, display, video, app, local and performance max.

Paying 1p per click is also possible with remarketing campaigns in less competitive industries. This is common with businesses that are within the Internet of Things (IoT) industries and want to retarget people to download a white paper or book a free demo.

Also, campaigns that focus on brand awareness and raising awareness like display and video campaigns, have very low average CPC costs in Google Ads. Because these campaigns are not focused on people who are searching, there tends to be less competition in the areas that they advertise in.

Keyword type

There are many different types of keywords. These include transactional, informational, brand, navigational, long tail, short tail and more. So, the type of keywords you select will determine the average Google Ads CPC rates.

Transactional keywords for both products and services are more competitive and so will be more expensive. There will be many advertisers bidding on them.

Informational searches are usually a lot less competitive, so you'll pay less, but you'll also see a low count in conversions. So, your return on ad spend will be low.

How to reduce your Google Ads CPC

Reducing your Google Ads cost per click (CPC) costs is one of the most important actions you could take in your account to improve performance. This is mainly because it also reduces your overall spend and means you need to have less budget to achieve the campaign goals you've set.

To do this effectively requires taking specific actions to make sure you're on your way to a good CPC rate. Some actions will be easier than others and some will require you to wait longer to see the results. So, how you go about it will depend on the bid strategies you're using and what campaigns you're running.

Below, I show you how to reduce your Google Ads CPC while helping you to achieve your goals.

Lower keyword bids

One of the quickest ways to reduce your Google Ads CPC is to lower your bids. Lowering your bids means you will have a cap on how much you'll pay for each ad click.

How you reduce your CPC bids depends on the bid strategy that you're currently using. For example, if you're using manual CPC bidding you can change the maximum CPC bid limit at the ad group or keyword levels.

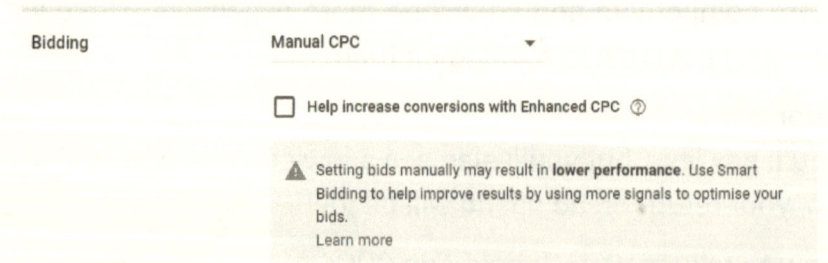

Just remember that if you're using eCPC bidding with your manual bidding you may still pay above the limit sometimes. This is because eCPC will bid higher if the system has determined that you're likely to get a conversion or bid lower if you're not likely to get a conversion.

If you're using an automated bid strategy, like maximise clicks, you can add a bid cap limit or reduce it if you have one. That means the system will now bid lower, but that may have a negative impact on the performance of your ads, so it's worth testing this as you run your ads.

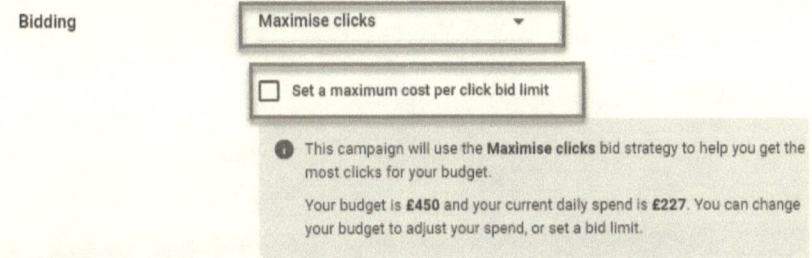

Add negative keywords

Adding negative keywords in your campaigns and ad groups helps you to block searches that are not relevant for your business. It also helps you to block searches that have high CPC rates and are not performing very well and costing you much.

It's far more important to check your CPCs at the search term level and not just the keyword level. This is because some searches will have high CPCs while some will have low ones, so looking at it at the keyword level does not give you much information about what is happening at the search level.

You can add negative keywords at the campaign or ad group levels. Or you can add them to a negative keyword list at the account level and then apply them to multiple campaigns.

Change bidding strategy

Changing your bid strategy is one effective way to reduce your Google Ads cost per click (CPC). For example, if you've been using an automated bid strategy, changing to a manual one will help you to have more control over your bids. you'll then reduce your bids and that will help to reduce your CPCs.

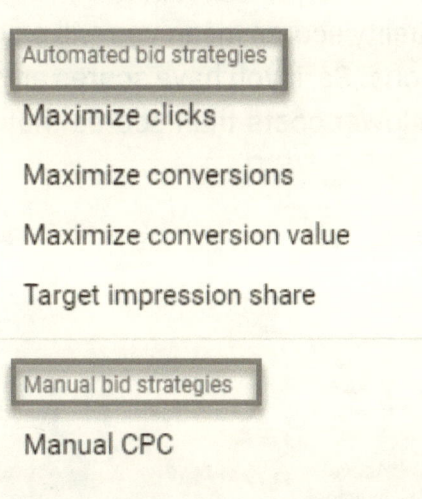

As mentioned above, manual CPC allows you to set bids at the keyword and ad group levels. you'll set a maximum CPC limit to prevent the system from bidding higher than that and that will help you to control the CPCs.

The actual CPC you pay is what is minimally required to clear the ad rank thresholds and beat the ad rank of the advertiser below you. If there are no other advertisers, you only pay a reserve price, which tends to be very low.

Also, using an automated bid strategy like maximise clicks allows you to put a bid cap to prevent the system from bidding higher.

Improve quality scores

A long-term approach to reducing your Google Ads CPC costs that reaps lasting results is to improve your keyword quality scores. Good quality scores mean you will pay less to achieve higher ad positions. So, if you have scores anywhere between 8-10, you'll see lower costs than scores that are below four, for example.

Quality Score	Exp. CTR	Ad relevance	Landing page exp.
10/10	Above average	Above average	Above average
10/10	Above average	Above average	Above average
10/10	Above average	Above average	Above average
9/10	Above average	Average	Above average

Poor quality scores mean you have to bid higher to appear in higher positions relative to your competitors. So, work on your landing page experience, ad relevance and expected click through rate to improve your quality scores.

Some actions that help include checking your website speed with PageSpeed Insights and following the guidelines there to fix it. Also, make sure your ads are highly relevant to your keywords and search terms.

Find long tail keywords

Adding long tail keywords helps you to target keywords that are less competitive, and less competitive always means you'll pay less for each click and will reduce the average CPC across your campaign.

This is because long tail keywords target long tail searches that are highly specific and are often ignored by many other advertisers.

You can look for long tail keywords by carrying out keyword research with the Keyword Planner tool. As you carry out this research, look for keywords with four words or more. There won't be that many, so you'll need to keep searching, but the few that you find that are relevant can be added to your campaign and bid on.

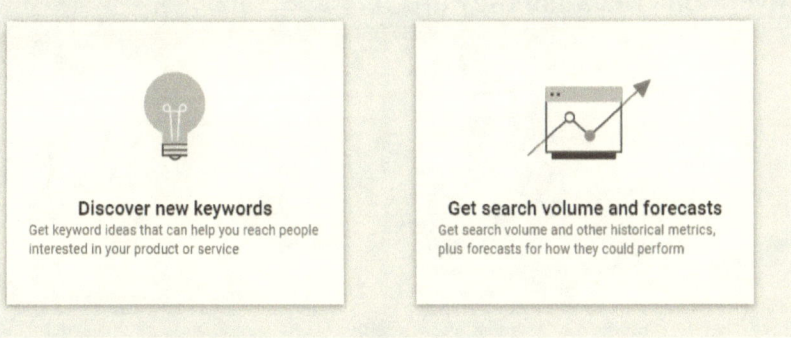

A great place to find long tail keywords is in the search terms report. When you see any relevant searches there, click and add them to your ad groups, and if you're using manual bidding, set a maximum CPC bid for them.

Use broad match type keywords

Adding broad match type keywords will send you a wide range of searches. Some of these will be less competitive and will lead to a drop in the average Google Ads CPC in your campaigns.

However, there are some problems associated with adding broad match keywords. The first is that you're likely to get some searches that are not relevant for your business, and that could waste some of your budget. So, you'll need to add them as negative keywords to make sure they don't appear again.

Adding broad match keywords also sends long tail searches as described above. Long tail searches usually have lower CPCs than short tail ones and, on average, they have higher conversions because they are very specific.

CHAPTER 6

Keyword Research

Setting up a successful PPC campaign

Google Ads keyword research is a key part of setting up successful PPC campaigns. It's one of the first things you'll do, and you should spend enough time researching to find the various ways that people search for your products or services.

Firstly, you should understand your customer's needs. Try to think of all the ways they'll search and make a list of popular keywords that you can use as part of your research.

Then, go over to the Keyword Planner tool to start the search. This is a free tool in your Google Ads account, and it will produce a lot of info about your keywords including:

- What traffic volumes they get each month
- Closely related keywords that you can add
- Suggested bids based on past performance
- How competitive they are – low, medium, or high competition
- What budgets you should consider setting
- Suggested campaign and ad group grouping according to themes

So, there's a lot you can get from your Google Ads keyword research and here are some reasons why it's important:

Find good keywords

Before doing the keyword research, it's simple to come up with up to three keywords that represent what you do. Most people can do this easily. However, you need a more extensive list to target the various ways that people search.

The Google Keyword Planner tool will help you find keywords to bid on. These keywords will be based on the products or services you sell, and they'll cover the various ways that people search on Google.

Some will not be relevant, of course, but it's important to identify them so you can add them as negative keywords. Negative keyword research is as important as keyword research because it reveals the searches that would be a waste of your budget.

Estimation of traffic volumes

Keyword research for Google Ads will show you the average number of monthly searches for your keywords. This shows how many impressions your ads would have received, and you can also work out the number of clicks based on bids and click through rates.

This helps with your Google Ads budget setting. It would be a challenge to know what budgets to assign to your campaigns without knowing the number of impressions and potential clicks you could get. The suggested bid also gives you an indication of the competition level. If the suggested bid is high, then you must assign a higher budget to get decent click volumes.

Estimation of costs

The Keyword Planner tool has an in-built forecasting tool. You should use this tool when you've created a good list of keywords and now need to know what costs you're likely to pay.

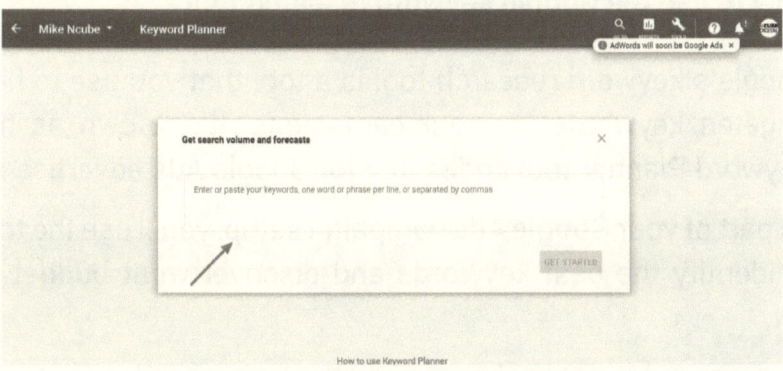

How to use Keyword Planner

You can adjust the bid for your keywords to see what the volume of clicks will be and at what cost. This helps you to plan your keyword strategy and to remove keywords that may prove too expensive at the beginning.

Discover competitors' strategy

Competitor tools aren't available in Google Ads, but there are some third-party tools like Spyfu and SE Ranking that will help you to spy on your competitors' ads and keywords.

You get a lot of information from these tools including:

- Top or bottom rankings for each keyword they are bidding on

- How much they are paying on average for each keyword
- What specific ads are showing for their keywords
- How much they are spending on their Google Ads campaigns
- What the competition levels are like for their keywords

How to use the Google keyword research tool

Google's keyword research tool is a tool that you use to find targeted keywords for your campaigns. It's known as the Keyword Planner tool and is free for Google Ads advertisers.

As part of your Google Ads campaign setup, you'll use the tool to identify the best keywords and discover what budget to set.

Here are some tips on how to use the Keyword Planner tool:

Add up to three keywords

First, start by choosing three keywords that your customers are likely to use when they search for your products or services. You'll need these to carry out the keyword research in the Keyword Planner tool.

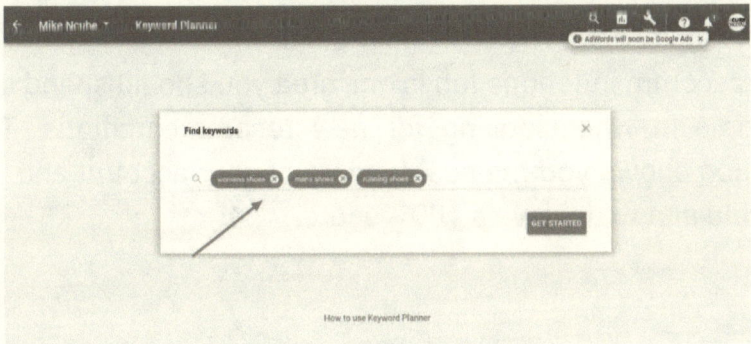

Add them in the tool and then click 'Get Started'. Next, add some negative keywords to block searches that are unlikely to be relevant. This will save you a lot of time from sifting through many irrelevant keywords and will save you a lot of money.

Add a landing page

You can also search your landing page or a competitor's one for keywords. Add the URL in the box, update the settings as mentioned above and then click the submit button.

The Keyword Planner tool will search the landing page for potential keywords, and you can add these in existing or new ad groups.

Choose the location

Next, enter the location you want to do research for. You can add one or more locations to get as many results as possible, but these should be relevant locations you want to target in your campaigns.

Check the recommendations tab

The recommendations tab is one area you should spend a lot of time in when looking for new recommendations. This section shows you the health score of your account and you should aim to achieve a 100% score.

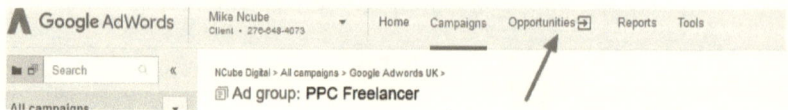

The recommendations tab is where you'll also get keyword suggestions. The Google Ads system suggests new keywords based on your ad groups and gives you an idea of how many clicks you'll get and at what cost.

Not all suggestions here will be relevant. Some will be vastly different from what you sell or promote but some will be keyword recommendations that you may not have thought of.

Use the forecasting tool

The forecasting tool is available in the Keyword Planner. If you have a list of keywords that you need to assess for potential volumes and costs, you can plug them into this tool and adjust the bids to see what you're likely to get back.

Note that this is just a forecast and actual performance may differ at auction time. Bear in mind that this tool won't help you find more keyword recommendations, but it will help you see how viable your current ones are.

You can then decide if you'd like to add them in your campaign or remove them altogether.

How many keywords should you have in each ad group?

There're several factors to how many keywords you should have in each ad group, and these will differ for every advertiser. It's important to have an idea of what you'd like to achieve before deciding how many keywords you should have.

The number of keywords you have in each ad group affects click through rates (CTR), quality scores and conversions. Getting this wrong can lead to campaign failure. These metrics should help you decide how many to include in each ad group.

First, you'll start with keyword research. That will inform you how many keywords to include in each group and how you will manage and optimise them.

Here are some tips to help you decide this:

A minimum five keywords

The Google system recommends that you have at least five keywords in each ad group. If you check the recommendations tab, you'll see suggestions to include more keywords in any ad groups that have fewer than five.

Adding more will push your search health score higher, and closer to 100%. Of course, these suggestions are based on Google's knowledge of your campaigns, and it will try to pick closely related keywords.

However, adding keywords just for the sake of it could harm your campaigns. Some keyword suggestions may not be relevant to the ad groups and that could affect conversions, CTR and quality scores.

Maximum 20 keywords

Don't add more than 20 keywords per ad group. You want to keep your ad groups tightly themed, and the fewer keywords you have, the better.

Too many keywords lead to low CTR and poor-quality scores. This is because it's difficult to have every keyword included in the ads.

Keywords should always be included in the ads. When people see their keyword in the ad, they're more likely to click, and this boosts overall performance.

Follow the rule of two

The rule of two states that every keyword in the ad group should have at least two primary words. It ensures that you don't add too many keywords and that they're all related to each other.

So, the keyword 'Hire Google Ads Expert' has at least two primary words 'Google Ads' and 'Expert'. Consequently, these two should be part of every keyword that's included in the ad group.

The following would also be closely related to it because they follow the 'rule of two':

- Google Ads Expert Help
- Google Ads Expert
- Google Ads Expert Support

- Find Google Ads Expert

However, some of these would be fine in their own ad groups. The point is that ad groups should be tightly themed, and all keywords should be related.

CHAPTER 7

Landing Pages

Pay per click (PPC) landing pages are pages where your visitors are taken to when they click on your ads. With most ad types in Google Ads and similar platforms, you'll need to add landing pages to direct your visitors to so they can complete the actions that are important for your business.

However, there are some ad formats that don't require PPC landing pages, like when you are running call only ads to drive calls only and when you're running a local campaign and promoting your Google Business Profile page.

But landing pages are very important for most advertisers because they help to drive a lot more traffic and conversions. Most advertisers that run campaigns without landing pages are usually at an early stage of advertising or have very small businesses that just want to drive few clicks and conversions.

However, for larger businesses and those that are more established, dedicated landing pages are important. They help to drive people to pages that have the information they need to complete an action that is important for your business.

Why use PPC landing pages?

Having PPC landing pages means you can direct visitors to specific pages that relate to the products or services you're promoting. This contrasts with using your homepage for example, which will usually have generic information about your business and not be specific enough.

PPC landing pages also help you to focus on one specific call to action that is important for the campaign you're running. So, if it's to get people to download a white paper, your ads can mention this on Google and the landing page should provide the download.

Using landing pages also increases engagement and ensures that your visitors get what they are looking for. Plus, you'll see metrics like conversion rate, bounce rate and others to improve for your business.

PPC landing pages for Google Ads

As a PPC platform, Google Ads is one of the most effective ways to promote your business. You can direct visitors from your ads to your website and landing pages by adding a final URL in your text ads and responsive display ads.

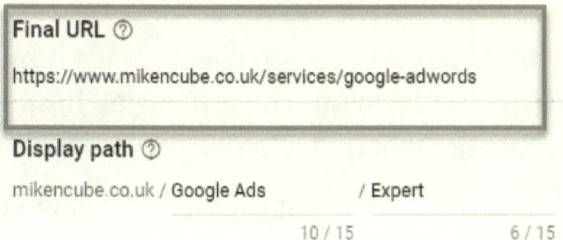

One of the things to consider is whether you'll use the landing pages on your website in Google Ads or use dedicated standalone pages to promote your products or services.

There are pros and cons to both. The advantages of using landing pages on your website is that they are usually quicker to create, and they also usually have more credibility because people sometimes want to check out your whole website to see who you really are. So, it helps to give them more confidence to convert, but one drawback with this is that they can easily get distracted by other pages on your website, and they can get pulled away from the main action you want them to complete.

Using standalone pages or a micro site has the benefit of getting your visitors to focus on one action that you want them to complete. For example, if you want to collect details and provide an investment service, this will help you to direct all visitors to that one action and nothing else.

The drawback to using standalone PPC landing pages is that this can lower your credibility. Quite often people want to see other pages to gain confidence that they are dealing with a real business, so you may lose some visitors.

PPC landing pages bounce rates

There are several metrics that you can check to see how your PPC landing pages are performing. These help you to see how engaged your visitors are when they arrive on your website.

Bounce rate is one of the important metrics. It helps you to quickly see the percentage of people that leave your website without viewing other pages, and this is important in helping you achieve good quality scores.

Source/Medium	Acquisition			Behaviour
	Users	New Users	Sessions	Bounce Rate
	2,659 % of Total: 100.00% (2,659)	2,576 % of Total: 100.00% (2,576)	3,375 % of Total: 100.00% (3,375)	80.74% Avg for View: 80.74% (0.00%)
1. google / organic	1,827 (68.27%)	1,790 (69.49%)	2,066 (61.21%)	85.43%
2. google / cpc	482 (18.01%)	441 (17.12%)	642 (19.02%)	88.63%
3. (direct) / (none)	247 (9.23%)	237 (9.20%)	456 (13.51%)	56.58%
4. bing / organic	48 (1.79%)	45 (1.75%)	49 (1.45%)	95.92%
5. baidu / organic	15 (0.56%)	15 (0.58%)	15 (0.44%)	100.00%
6. yahoo / organic	9 (0.34%)	9 (0.35%)	10 (0.30%)	100.00%
7. elearning.digitally-smart.com / referral	6 (0.22%)	6 (0.23%)	6 (0.18%)	83.33%
8. m.facebook.com / referral	5 (0.19%)	5 (0.19%)	5 (0.15%)	100.00%

Aim to achieve bounce rates below 50%. There are several steps that will help you to achieve this as you analyse your bounce rates in Google Ads. Make sure your pages are well optimised and load quickly, which you can check with the PageSpeed Insights tool.

A Google search console account will help you to see if there are any errors, and you can work with your web developer to fix them.

What factors make up landing page quality score in Google Ads?

Landing page experience is one of the three factors to your keyword quality scores. It reveals how engaged visitors are on your website and if they're finding what they're looking for.

So, it's important that you send visitors to the correct landing pages and that they are fully optimised to keep them engaged and purchasing.

Get the free Google Ads Guide to Increase Sales & Leads.

There are several actions you can take to improve your landing pages, and these include:

Fast loading pages

A fast-loading page is essential to a great user experience. People won't stick around if your pages are slow and take time to load. They'll click the back button or close the website altogether and go to a competitor's website that offers a great experience, and you'll have lost them forever.

Fast load times are especially important for mobiles. With over 50% of searches now taking place on mobiles and with people 'on the go', it's critical that your pages load quickly.

Fully mobile-responsive pages

With mobile searches now being so important, it's vital that visitors have a great experience. There should be no distractions or delays as they browse on the go, and all pages should be responsive and easily navigable.

Having a mobile-specific site is helpful and providing an app will provide a great user experience. However, smartphones now have bigger screens, load faster and it's possible to complete all tasks as you would on a desktop.

Bounce rate

A bounce is when a visitor leaves your website without viewing other pages, so that's considered a 100% bounce. You should aim to reduce your average bounce rate below 50%.

If visitors leave your website without taking any action like viewing another page, this will affect your landing page scores. This is because it will lead to a high bounce rate.

This is a sign of low engagement, so you should increase it by sending visitors to the right landing pages and ensure that your landing page delivers on the promise made in the ad. Doing so will bring the landing page experience to the 'Above Average' status.

Website content

This is the most important factor to a landing page's quality score. The text, images and calls to action should all be aligned to the users' needs and should fulfil the promise made in the ad.

Also, ensure that you include the primary keywords on the page. This includes in H1 and H2 tags, the body text and alt text of the images. Doing so helps to improve its relevance and users will spend more time on the page and complete the actions you want them to.

Ways to improve your Google Ads landing pages

A Google Ads landing page is a page on your website that visitors reach when they click one of your pay per click (PPC) ads. Its goal is to deliver on what your ad has promised the visitor and should provide a great user experience for them, too.

A landing page experience is one of the three main factors behind your quality scores. If you have high bounce rates and low visitor engagement, this will show in your quality scores as a 'Below Average' landing page experience.

Also, a poor landing page experience for your Google Ads visitors means you are unlikely to achieve good conversion rates that would make advertising on Google worth it.

So, here are 10 tips to help optimise your landing page experience and boost your Google Ads campaigns:

Avoid popups

If you can, avoid adding popups, especially if they are not in line with the content on the landing page. Popups can be annoying for users and are usually not relevant for PPC campaigns because everything the visitor needs should be available on the landing page in most cases.

Also, Google will disapprove ads if a popup distracts visitors and is not relevant to the ads and keywords.

A popup can be ok if you would like to highlight a special offer, like a discount that's related to the product or service on the landing page. In fact, this can lead to higher conversion rates because it can be a strong incentive for visitors.

Also, popups are more of an annoyance on mobile devices because they are harder to close. One option is to have it appear for your desktop visitors and not mobile visitors. Mobile visitors usually have less time and patience and will quickly click the back button if they are obstructed.

Remove all distractions

Don't stop your visitors from doing what they have arrived on your landing page to do. Remember, they have clicked one of your PPC ads and you have been charged by Google. This should motivate you to make the experience as best as possible.

One common distraction is having too much text on a landing page. Most visitors don't read website text, but just scan through it to pick the most important points. So, if you have too much text on the page, then that could be off-putting for many people and will make it difficult for them to scan and find what they need.

Popups and banners can be distractions too and should be avoided at all costs. If you must add them, they should be kept to a minimum and relevant to the page content and offers.

Add a call to action

A call to action is a definite must for all your PPC landing pages. The call to action on your ad should be the same one your visitors see on the landing page. So, if the ad has promised a white paper download, this should be available on the landing page, without the visitor having to search the website for it.

Also, the call to action should be visible 'Above the fold', which is what visitors see as soon as they land on the page.

This is especially important on mobile devices which are harder to navigate than desktop. Your conversion rates will be higher when the call to action is visible at the top, on mobile devices – without them having to scroll down to see the call to action.

Many features can act as a call to action, and these include a phone number, banner, email, form, button, and others.

Use software like Hotjar

Hotjar is an amazing analytics platform that was developed in 2014 to help you analyse your website traffic, receive feedback, carry out surveys and do much more to optimise your website and landing pages.

One of the best features is the recording of website visitors' actions, which gives you the 'big picture' of how to improve your site's user experience and performance or conversion rates.

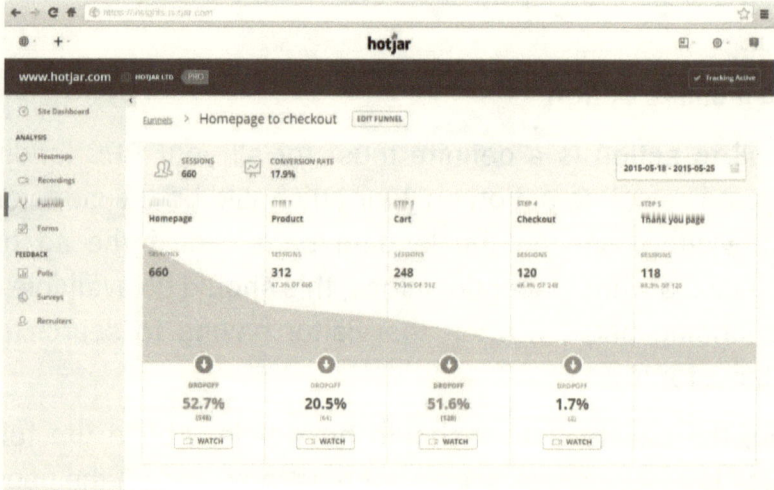

Use white space

Break up your text with white space to make it easier for your visitors to scan or read easily. There is nothing as off putting on a landing page as large chunks of paragraphs with very little white space in between.

Visitors will find it hard to digest your content and will completely ignore anything that looks difficult to read. So, you will fail to get your key points across and completely lose them to competitor sites that have well-structured content.

Add reviews

You are at a great disadvantage if your competitors have reviews and your landing pages do not. Many website visitors will be looking for proof of your expertise or past performance from reviews – and without them, you will find it difficult to convince them of that fact.

There are many credible third-party review sites like Trustpilot and Feefo, and for a small monthly fee, you can collect customer reviews. This will be a great investment for your business.

Have an 'About Us' page

Many of your visitors will be looking for an 'About Us' page to learn more about your business before they decide to trade with you. It still amazes me to find many sites don't have an 'About Us' page as this is one of the most basic features to add.

Having the 'About Us' page visible from any of your landing pages will make it easy for your visitors to learn about your business. After reading that and having gained more confidence, they will return to the landing page to complete a conversion.

Add a contact form

A contact form is a must if you want to turn visitors into leads. People are more likely to contact you if you have a well-designed and targeted form on the landing page.

It's especially important for mobile visitors who can fill out the form quickly and move on to whatever else they need to do.

Of course, you should have a separate contact page for visitors who want to use that, however, including the form on the landing page will help to boost user experience and conversions too.

Have a 'Thank you' page

It's better to have a 'Thank you' page for your contact form than an in-line thank you message. A 'Thank you' page helps to reduce bounce rates for your website and increases the overall visitor experience.

You can also use the 'Thank you' page to set expectations for your visitors about when you will get back to them. This is more difficult with an in-line message, which will normally just say 'Thank you for contacting us. We will contact you shortly'.

Again, with a 'Thank You' page, you can promote other areas of your website and even offer a white paper download or eBOOK which they can read to learn more about your business.

Finally, a 'Thank You' page makes tracking your Google Ads traffic a lot easier. With an in-line message, you would have to setup event tracking, which can be tricky to set up at the best of times. With the 'Thank You' page, all you need is the URL which you will use to set up goal tracking in Google Analytics and track your PPC traffic easily.

Update your footer

Your footer represents the end of the line for your landing page visitor. They have read your content and have reached the bottom of the page but are not sure what to do next.

This is where you can promote other pages on your website by adding links to those pages. You can also add a newsletter signup or a contact form to make it easy for them to contact you.

CHAPTER 8

Match Types

Keyword match types in Google Ads help you control the type of searches your ads appear for. There are four Google Ads match types: broad, phrase, exact match, and negative match.

You can add one or more in your campaigns according to your requirements and goals. For example, when first setting up a Google Ads campaign, it's probably best to start with 'phrase' and 'exact match' type keywords. Later, you can add 'modified broad' and then 'broad' to extend your reach.

As a Google Ads expert, I use a wide range of keywords and all match types in the campaigns I launch. I also run my own campaigns and I'll use a keyword that I bid on, 'Google Ads Freelancer', to illustrate how match types work.

Broad match

Broad match is the default match type in Google Ads. When you first add keywords in your campaign, they'll be broad match type keywords and they won't have any designations like other match types.

Broad match type drives a wide range of searches. It's the only match type that matches to synonyms of your keywords. For example, a keyword like 'Google Ads Specialist' will match with 'Google Ads expert' and other similar synonyms.

Like other match types, it also matches with close variants, stemmings, plurals or singulars, abbreviations, misspellings and so on.

Phrase match

Phrase match triggers ads for searches that match a phrase or a close variation of it with additional words before or after. However, ads won't show if a word is added to the middle of the phrase.

It's designated with quotation marks as the following keyword 'Google Ads Freelancer'. This keyword would match for a search like 'Google Ads Freelancer London', but it would not appear for a search that has a word in the middle such as 'Google Ads Top Freelancer'.

Exact match

Ads are only shown for the exact searches or close variations of them. Close variations include the reordering of the words if the meaning is not lost.

This match type is designated with brackets as the following [Google Ads Freelancer].

Which keyword match types should I use in Google Ads?

The keyword match types you use are important to the success of your campaigns. Whether you're launching new Google Ads campaigns or are looking to update or change match types, you should understand the implications of the change.

About 15% of searches each day are completely new to Google, so it's important to understand how match types work.

Match types are divided into two main types: semantic and syntactic. Semantic refers to the meaning of words and is related to broad match type keywords and the meaning of those searches. So, it's common to appear for synonyms unlike the other three match types.

Syntactic is about the arrangement of words regardless of their meaning and is related to phrase, exact and modified broad match types. These types of keywords only appear for close variants, plurals, singulars, acronyms and stemmings but not for synonyms.

I'll illustrate how each match type works with the keyword 'Google Ads Expert':

Broad match

Broad match type is broad in its reach. It drives a wide range of searches for your ads and keywords which include plurals, singulars, synonyms, acronyms, stemmings, misspellings and more.

It's often not best to start with a broad match type. This is because you're unlikely to have built an extensive negative keyword list at launch to block irrelevant searches.

Instead, look to add broad match type keywords when you want to increase click volume and target longer tail keywords.

The broad match keyword for 'Google Ads Expert' will trigger such searches:

- Google Ads Expert (Exact)
- Expert in Google Ads (in any order and other words included)
- Google Ads Specialist (Synonym)
- Add words in Google (not relevant search term)

So, you see how some may not be relevant and how some are synonyms. It's important to know this and factor it in as you do keyword research.

Phrase match

Phrase match keywords are enclosed in quotation marks, like "Google Ads Expert". These target searches that have words in that same order and can have words before or after that keyword. So, the keywords above will match with searches like:

- Google Ads Expert
- Hire Google Ads Expert
- Google Ads Expert in Milton Keynes

Phrase match keywords give you more control over the searches your ads appear for than modified broad matches, so you're often sure of what you'll see in the search terms report. In most cases, you'll not see big surprises but it's still important to have relevant negative keywords in place.

Exact Match

Exact match keywords are enclosed in brackets like [Google Ads Expert]. So, they only match to exact matches including close variants including plurals/singulars, misspellings and similar. The searches should also be in the exact same order, so the keyword [Google Ads Expert] will match to:

- Google Ads Expert (exact)
- Google Ads Experts (plural)
- Google Ads Espert (misspelling)

The exact match keyword [Google Ads Expert] will not match for the following:

- Google Ads Specialist

So, pick your keyword match types wisely and focus on your goals and how they'll help you achieve them.

CHAPTER 9

Negative Keywords

Building a good negative keyword list is a must if you want to run successful PPC campaigns. Your list should be built over the lifetime of your campaigns, and you should continue to update it to keep it in line with performance.

There are several ways to add negative keywords in your account. You can add them at the account, campaign, or ad group level.

At the campaign and ad group level, you can add them individually or in bulk. This is quick and easy, and you can do it in your search terms report when you find searches that aren't relevant.

At the account level, you add them in the Shared Library for negative keywords, under the 'Tools' section. First you create a list and then add the negative keywords and then you can apply it to as many campaigns as you like.

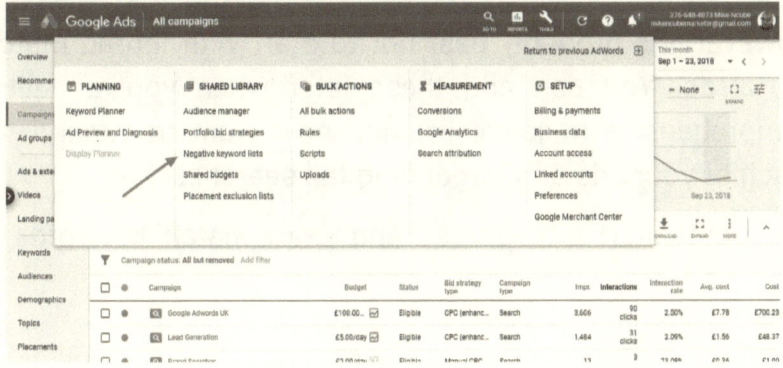

Creating a negative keyword list this way will save you a lot of time. You won't have to add keywords manually into each campaign and you can do it in bulk in the Shared Library.

Here's how you can build a negative keyword list:

Keyword Planner tool

The Keyword Planner tool is a free tool in your Google Ads account. You can find it under the 'Tools' section and use it to conduct keyword research for your campaigns.

As you search for keywords, you'll identify some keywords that aren't relevant for your products or services. So, you can also collect these and add them as negative keywords at the account, campaign, or ad group level.

It's important to do this especially if you're using match types. For example, if you have broad match keywords, your keywords will drive a wide range of searches, many of which will not be relevant.

This is common when a campaign is new and has just been launched, so you can help prevent some budget wastage by adding negative keywords.

However, it's probably best not to start with 'broad match' keywords. You can add these later when you've built a comprehensive negative list and now want to expand the reach of your ads and target long tail searches.

It's best to start with 'phrase' and 'exact match' keywords.

Search terms report

Next, to build your negative keyword list, you need to regularly check your search terms report. You should do this on a weekly or monthly basis as you manage and optimise your PPC campaigns.

The search terms report is one of the most important reports for your search and shopping campaigns. It reveals to you the actual searches that are leading to clicks on your ads.

Since you'll have different keyword match types, you will have a wide range of long tail searches in your reports, and you'll find words that aren't relevant for your products or services in these reports.

Brainstorming

One of the important places to search for negative keywords is in your head. As an expert in your industry, you will know a lot about your customers and what they want and don't want. You'll know the potential and limitations of your products or services, so you'll be able to come up with a few negatives just by brainstorming. For example, if you're promoting a service, you'll not want people searching for jobs and you'll add words such as:

- Jobs
- Careers
- CV and other similar keywords

These are easy to come up with and you can add them early on.

When to add negative keywords in Google Ads

Adding negative keywords in Google Ads is a task you should do regularly. It helps you reduce wasted budget and makes your ads more effective in reaching the right people.

Here are some tips on when you should add negative keywords in Google Ads:

Keyword research

The first time to add negative keywords is when you do keyword research. This will be at the very beginning of your advertising and keyword research will be one of the first things you'll do.

You'll start by brainstorming some keywords that you'll use as part of the research. With your knowledge of your industry, products, or services, this shouldn't be too hard.

If, on the other hand, you're setting up a campaign for a client, then you should request this from them. You'll then carry out the keyword research, and as you do so, you'll find negative keywords to add to the campaign.

You can carry out competitor research with a tool like Spyfu to see what keywords they are bidding on and find some potential negatives.

Campaign launch

After doing keyword research and having built a good list of negative keywords, you should now add them before launching your campaign. You will also get recommendations for other keywords as you work on your ad groups. You'll find some aren't relevant and you can add these in the negative list.

Campaign management

Throughout the management of your Google Ads account, you'll need to add negative keywords. You'll do this to block searches that aren't relevant for your business.

The search terms report is the most important report to help you do this. In this report, you'll see a wide range of searches, and some won't be relevant.

It's common to see newly launched campaigns that have over 10% of searches that aren't relevant. So, if that is not fixed, you could be wasting a lot of money on these irrelevant searches.

Some searches may look relevant, but if they have poor conversions, then you should consider adding them as negative keywords – especially if they've received over 100 clicks each.

7 reasons why you should add negative keywords

Negative keywords help improve your campaigns immensely. As you launch and run Google Ads campaigns, it's inevitable that you'll get some searches that aren't relevant, and you'll need to block them.

Adding negative keywords has many benefits, and these include:

- Less wasted budget
- Increases conversion rates

- Increases sales
- Reduces cost per conversion
- Improves click through rates
- Reduces bounce rates
- Improves profitability

So, let's dive deeper into the seven reasons why you should add negative keywords:

Reducing wasted budget

Negative keywords block searches that eat into your budget with no return. Considering how advertising budgets are always being squeezed, it's important that every penny is well spent and is contributing to conversions.

Budget setting is one of the most important tasks in Google Ads and having a sufficient one is crucial. So, you can help your budget go further by reducing any wastage.

Increased conversion rates

With more budget going to better performing keywords, this leads to better conversion rates, and it's possible to get conversion rates that are higher than 5%.

The conversion rate is a metric you track in your campaigns. You can see it for your ads, keywords, and ad groups, so you can easily track and improve it in your campaigns by adding poor performing search terms as negative keywords.

Increased sales for targeted keywords

Better conversion rates lead to increased sales for the available budget.

Adding negative keywords means you block all irrelevant searches and give relevant ones more budget to perform better. Your best keywords are then likely to get more clicks and conversions if budget was limited before.

More sales also mean an account that is more successful because search terms are very important to campaigns. They should be managed regularly and blocked if they aren't relevant.

Reduced cost per conversion

With a good list of negative keywords which leads to increased sales for your budget, you'll see an improvement in cost per conversion. This will reduce the cost for each conversion you get, so you'll be able to add more budget in your campaigns.

Cost per conversion is one of the key metrics in your account and you can see it for your ads, keywords, ad groups and campaigns. So, it's easy to track and analyse, and therefore, improve.

Improved click through rates

In your search terms report, you can see which searches have low click through rates. If you find any with low CTRs and poor performance, you should add them as negative keywords/terms.

You can do this easily by selecting them and adding them as negatives at the campaign or ad group level.

Reduced bounce rates

Adding negative keywords that have low engagement will help to improve bounce rates. A high bounce rate that is above 60% is an indication that a visitor is not engaged, so if that's a trend you see with specific keywords, then you should block them with negative keywords.

Increased profitability

Finally, adding negative keywords helps to improve profitability, the most important goal of advertising.

CHAPTER 10

Quality Scores

Quality scores are Google's diagnostic tool that advertisers use to create a great experience for their users.

It's a score between 1-10 that's assigned to keywords in your account. Improving this score for each of your keywords helps to create a great user experience, which benefits users, advertisers, and Google, too.

You can see the quality score for your keywords in the status section of each keyword. You'll also be able to see how they score for the factors that contribute to your quality scores.

Google's advice to advertisers is to give your users what they are looking for and a great quality score will follow. The Google Ads system is set up to reward quality ads with a higher ad rank for less cost.

Next are some important facts about quality scores.

Quality score facts
It is based on exact match keywords

The 1-10 scale estimates your quality score for a search that matches your keyword exactly. So, any long tail searches that aren't exactly matched will not impact your scores. It doesn't reflect match types or negative keywords that you may have added. Although negative keywords are a good thing for your account, quality scores don't include them as a factor.

It contributes to ad rank

Your quality score is one of two factors that affect ad rank. The other factor is your keyword bid. Ad rank determines where your ad will be positioned in the auction result. This can be in one of the top four positions above the organic results or one of the bottom three on the first page results. So, ad rank is important, and you should work on your quality scores to improve it.

It is a diagnostic tool

The quality scores are a helpful diagnostic tool and not a performance indicator. Its aim is to alert you to any potential problems in your account that need to be fixed. It works like the warning lights in your car which alert you to any potential problems in your vehicle's engine or other parts.

It is a keyword metric

A quality score is a metric for keywords only; it is not a campaign, ad group, ad, or account metric. So, you won't see a quality score for your ads or ad groups, and neither will you see it for your search terms. You'll only see it reported for the keywords in your account. Each keyword that has been active and received traffic will display a score, and you can see it in the status column.

It is not a key performance indicator

The quality scores are not a key performance indicator (KPI). So, although it's an important metric that helps you identify any potential problems, its role is not to determine all optimisations that take place in your account.

It is calculated at auction time

The quality scores are only calculated when your ads are eligible to appear in the auction results. Your keywords will not have quality scores if they've never appeared in a search auction and/or if they've not matched to the exact match of your keywords. New keywords and those that have not appeared in an auction will have a null quality score, meaning they will not have a score and you'll see the designation '-' next to the keyword.

It should be improved

You should work on quality scores because this helps the overall performance of your account. Achieving a quality score of 10/10 for all keywords should be the goal. Getting close to this will ensure that you are meeting the needs of searchers and future customers for your business. You should work on each of the three factors below to improve your quality scores.

It is affected by the landing page experience

The landing page experience is a quality score feature. Improving it helps to improve quality scores and other metrics like conversions. This feature will have one of three statuses: below average, average, or above average. So, if it is showing as below average or average, you should take action to improve this. This includes optimising your landing pages to increase engagement and reduce bounce rates.

It is affected by expected CTR

This is the second factor to your quality scores. Expected click through rate (CTR) is determined by factors such as the search query, the device used, location, actual CTR, etc. So, ensuring that your targeting is precise is important. Make sure that your ads are well written and encourage visitors to click through to your website.

It is affected by ad relevance

Another factor to your quality scores like the two mentioned above, will have a status of below average, average, or above average. This is the most important of all three because relevance is great for everyone: searchers, advertisers, and Google. Ad Relevance is about making sure that Ads are highly targeted to users and are related to the keywords you've added in your ad groups.

Not an account or campaign metric

As mentioned earlier, there's no such thing as an account or campaign quality scores. This is only reported for keywords that have been or are active and receiving traffic. So, the quality scores for one keyword doesn't affect another, and neither does it affect the overall performance of your account or campaigns. Also, if you move keywords to another ad group or campaign and don't change the ads and landing pages, quality scores will not change.

New keywords have null quality scores

When you add new keywords, they'll have a null quality score designated with '-' . In the past, Google Ads would assign an automatic 6/10 for new keywords but they've since changed this. The null score makes sense considering that quality scores are only calculated when a keyword is active and receiving traffic.

Check historical quality scores

You can add historical quality score columns in your keyword reports. Historical quality scores show you how it has changed for your keywords over time. This historical data will be available for the three quality scores factors: landing page experience, ad relevance, expected CTR, and quality score. This will show the statuses for each of them.

How you structure your account doesn't matter

How you structure your account and campaigns doesn't affect quality scores. You can structure your campaigns in a way that makes it easy for you to manage your ads. So, if it doesn't affect the user's experience, then it shouldn't affect quality scores. You should setup your PPC campaigns in whatever way will allow you to manage them best. There's no such thing as an ad group, campaign, or account level quality score.

Running ads on another network doesn't matter

Running ads on other networks like the Google Display Network or search partners in your search campaigns will not impact quality scores. Quality scores are only calculated for keywords that trigger ads on Google websites.

Your ad position doesn't affect quality scores

While it's great to have high ad positions, doing so doesn't impact quality scores in any way. This is because the expected CTR, which is one of the quality scores' factors, is normalised for your actual position in the auction results. Top ads are generally expected to have a higher CTR and more clicks than lower positioned ads. This is also normalised for other factors which affect visibility such as ad extensions and other ad formats.

You don't need to bid higher to improve quality scores

This also means you don't need to bid higher to improve quality scores. Bidding higher may improve your ad position and increase CTRs and clicks, but it won't impact expected CTR and quality scores. So, you're free to bid for performance to improve clicks, conversions, and costs and what works for your business.

Have 3-5 ads per ad group to improve quality scores

You should add between 3-5 ads per ad group. This is great for testing different features and benefits in your ads and improves ad relevance, one of the main components of your quality scores. You should allow the Google Ads machine learning system to rotate the ads and then give more prominence to the ads that have the best performance.

Add dynamic keyword insertion in ads

Adding dynamic keyword insertion (DKI) in your ads helps to make them more relevant to searches. This syntax helps increase click through rates (CTRs) which affects expected

CTR, one of the components of quality scores. Adding DKI ensures that the keywords people use to find your website will appear in the ad and they are more likely to click.

The user's device is important

The device that a user uses to search is important. Whether it's a desktop, tablet or mobile, their experience will differ and the experience they have on your website will be different, too. So, it's important to ensure that user experience is great on all device types that you're targeting.

How important is a quality score?

The quality score is a diagnostic tool that reveals the health of your ads and landing pages. It's reported for every keyword in your account that has had sufficient impressions and clicks.

So, any keyword that has not run, or has had few impressions and clicks, won't have a quality score. Instead, it will be reported as a null quality score.

Generally, quality scores above 6 are good and reveal that the ads and landing pages are optimised. 10/10 quality scores are excellent and are what you should be aiming for.

When a user's experience is good, it then becomes good for everyone: advertisers, Google, and the users, too.

There're three main factors to quality score which you should work on improving:

- Expected click through rate (CTR)
- Ad relevance

- Landing page experience

Each of these factors is more important than the quality score number that you see for the keyword. The quality score is an aggregate of these three factors and doesn't tell you as much as each of the contributing factors.

Google is always looking for ways to improve the way that the quality score is calculated. That calculation will never be captured by a simple one -10 scale – which is why they call it a guide and not a precise metric.

There are other factors that contribute to ad quality that aren't directly reflected in the quality score. These are:

- Geographic signals – the country of the search will affect ad quality.
- User's device – the device, whether it's a desktop, tablet or mobile, will determine ad quality. This is considered when ad quality is calculated and it's important that your site is optimised for mobile visitors. Try targeting mobile visitors with specific mobile-friendly ads and pages.

What's a good keyword quality score?

A good quality score is good for everyone: users, advertisers, and Google, too. By deploying effective ads and keywords in tightly themed ad groups, you're more likely to reach 10/10 quality scores.

To improve your quality scores, you'll need to work on all three factors that contribute to its calculation: expected CTR, ad relevance and landing page experience. Each of these factors will have a performance status of below average, average, or above average.

Your goal should be to improve each of these to above average. Doing so will bring your keywords up to the 10/10 score.

Low quality score

A score below 5 is low and should be improved immediately. If you have keywords with quality scores between 1-4 you should look at the primary factors to see how they can be improved.

Low quality scores mean your ads will under-perform, and you'll have to bid higher to secure a high ad rank. This can be costly and could affect your profitability.

Quality scores of 1, for example, means your keywords have below average status for expected CTR, ad relevance and the landing page experience. You'll need to work on each factor to improve the quality score and overall performance of your ad campaign.

Average quality score

A quality score of 5 or 6 is average and one of the quality scores factors will be below average and will require fixing. Take time to understand why this is and make changes that will improve quality scores.

However, any changes you make should take conversion metrics into consideration. If you make changes to improve quality scores but don't factor in sales and leads you could affect performance.

Good quality score

A quality score of 7 or 8 is good. It's a reflection of relevant ads, a good click through rate and a good landing page experience. To achieve this, you would have to achieve above average for at least two factors and average for one.

Excellent quality score

An excellent quality scores is 9 or 10 and reveals that ads are of a high quality and landing pages are fully optimised. To achieve this, you should move all ads and keywords into tightly themed ad groups and ensure that searches are related to the keywords you're bidding on.

How to check keyword quality score in Google Ads

Checking keyword quality scores in Google Ads is easy. You have two places to check them and they're both in the keyword data table. You can view them here for each keyword or you can customise the data report to view them all at once.

So, here's how you can check your quality scores in Google Ads:

Check keywords status column

Next to each keyword, you'll see its status that you can hover your mouse over to see its quality score. This shows you what the keyword quality score is out of 10, with one being the lowest and 10 the highest.

Keyword ↑	Campaign	Ad group	Status
but removed keywords			
+adwords +contractor	Google Adwords UK	Adwords Contractor	Eligible
+adwords +expert	Google Adwords UK	Adwords Expert	Eligible
+adwords +expert	Call Only Campaign	Adwords Expert	Campaign paused

You also see the three factors to quality score calculation:

- Expected click through rate (CTR)
- Ad relevance
- Landing page experience

Next to each of these you'll see its status: below average, average, or above average. Each factor that has either below average or average status should be fixed.

If the landing page experience, for example, is below average or average, you should look at the factors causing this. Are you sending visitors to a generic page? Does the page have sufficient content? Are some keywords included in the page? Have you included some important elements such as a call to action?

Quality score status columns

In the keyword table, you can add quality score status columns. This helps you to see the scores for each of your keywords without hovering your mouse over each keyword, which can be time consuming.

These optional columns can be added in your keyword reports. You can arrange them from highest to lowest quality scores to easily assess them.

The status columns show the four quality score values:

- Quality score
- Landing page experience
- Ad relevance
- Expected CTR

Quality Score	Exp. CTR	Ad relevance	Landing page exp.
10/10	Above average	Above average	Above average
10/10	Above average	Above average	Above average
10/10	Above average	Above average	Above average
9/10	Above average	Average	Above average
	Above	Above	

As you can see in the image above, the three factors to quality scores each has a status of above average, average and below average.

Historical quality score status columns

The historical quality score status column is like the standard column above except that it reports on historical quality scores.

Quality Score (hist.)	Ad relevance (hist.)	Landing page exp. (hist.)	Exp. CTR (hist.)
–	–	–	–
5/10	Above average	Average	Below average
7/10	Above average	Average	Average
–	–	–	–
7/10	Above average	Above average	Below average
–	–	–	–

It reflects the last known scores for the reporting period. If you add the day segment to your reports, it will display the values that reflect what your quality score was at the end of each day.

However, the historical column will not report for dates before 22 January 2016, except if you've used a third-party app or scripts to download the historical quality score data.

5 tips to improve keyword quality scores

Anyone who's managed Google Ads campaigns knows that improving the quality scores can be a challenge. There're many factors that go into its calculation and they can each take a while to improve.

If you have scores as low as one or two and are looking to increase them to 10/10, you'll have to make some major changes to ads, keywords, and search terms.

Your keywords will have no quality scores when you first launch your Google Ads campaign. You'll see this when you hover your mouse over the speech bubble next to your keywords. This will be updated as your campaign starts to run, and your keywords are getting significant traffic volumes.

There're four main factors to your quality scores. These are landing page experience, expected CTR, ad relevance and ad extensions. Improving each of these will bring your scores to the 10/10 mark.

The primary factors to quality scores are landing page experience, expected CTR and ad relevance. they'll each have a status of below average, average, or above average to signify how optimised they are.

Here are five tips to improve quality scores for your keywords:

Improve landing pages

Landing pages are where people go when they've clicked your ads. They should be relevant to the search terms they've used and the keywords in the ad groups, and they should have the offer you've promised in the ad.

So, landing page experience is an important quality score factor. You want to make sure that the bounce rates are low, and that people are engaged when they're on your website.

To reduce bounce rates, you should get visitors to see other related pages. So, if you want people to contact you, make sure you add a contact form which sends them to a 'Thank you' page when they've clicked the 'Submit' button.

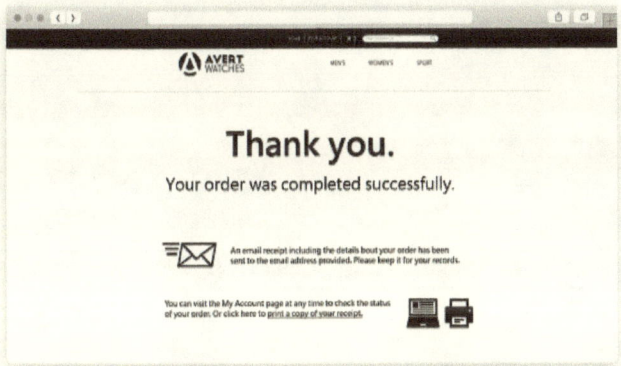

Doing this will reduce bounce rates. You can keep visitors more engaged by providing another related offer on the 'Thank you' page that moves them further down the buying funnel.

It also helps to set expectations. You can state on the landing page when they can expect to hear back from you and how you'll be contacting them.

On the other hand, if you've got a contact form, and all people see when they click the 'Submit' button is an in-line message that says something like 'Thanks for your message' you'll need to change this and add a 'Thank you' page.

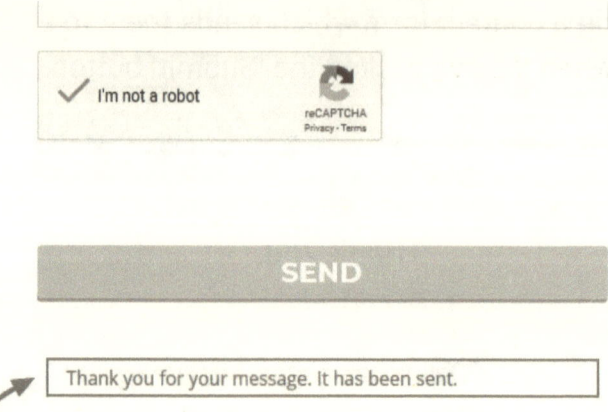

Increase click through rate

The click through rate formula is displayed as a percentage and is calculated by dividing clicks by impressions.

$$CTR = \frac{Clicks}{Impressions}$$

It's a measure of how targeted your ads are. If ads are targeted at the right audiences, then you'll see good CTRs. That will depend on your industry of course and it will vary for different keyword types.

However, 5% is usually a good CTR. That means for every 100 people that see your ads, five will click through to your website. Other factors will come into play, too, like competitors and their offers and where you're ranking in the ad auction results.

However, the quality score is decided by expected CTR and it forecasts what the CTR will be based on past performance, device used, search terms used, location of searcher and others.

There're several ways to improve the click through rate, including:

- Ensuring that the keyword is included in the ad, and the headline in particular
- Using the dynamic keyword insertion syntax to include the keyword in the ad automatically
- Removing ads, keywords, and search terms with low CTRs
- Removing broad match type keywords
- Removing one-word keywords that are underperforming

Make ads relevant

Making ads relevant is the most important factor when improving quality scores. When people search and see that the ad is what they've been looking for, they'll click through to learn more.

Google is serious about ad relevance. Over the years, they've updated the algorithms to reward ads that are relevant to searches. Quality scores are one of the most important metrics that they've implemented to show how relevant ads are to keywords.

Ad relevance is about ensuring the following:

- The keyword used is included in the ad text
- The product or service searched for is mentioned in the ad

- All relevant ad extensions have been added
- Character space is all used

Add ad extensions

Ad extensions give your ad more prominence in the search results. Your ad gets more space when you include all sitelinks, callouts, call, price, structured snippet, and location extensions that are applicable.

People are more likely to click through when your ad is at the top. This increases your CTR and quality score.

```
Adwords Freelancer | Exceptional Campaign Setup
[Ad] www.mikencube.co.uk/Adwords/Expert ▼
#1 UK Adwords Freelance Expert With Over 11 Years PPC Experience. Call Me.
Services: Adwords Setup, Adwords Management, SEO Copywriting, Digital Marketing, SEO
Adwords Management - from £100.00/mo - Monthly Management - More ▼
⦿ Luminous House, 300 South Row, Milton Keynes

    Client Reviews                        Awards & Certifications
    See What Past Clients Have To Say     See My AdWords & Marketing Awards
    About My Adwords PPC Service.         & Certifications From 2014-2016.
```

Target the right search terms

Targeting the right search terms helps to boost your keyword quality scores. If the search terms aren't related to your ads and the products or services you're promoting, then quality scores will be low.

There's a difference between a keyword and a search term. A keyword is what you add in your campaign to target people who are looking for your products or services. A search term on the other hand is what people use to find your products or services. The match types are what match your ads to the users search term.

Keyword match types control the search terms which will trigger your ads. The four match types you can use are broad, modified broad, phrase and exact match

Each ad group can have one or more keyword match types. When you first launch your PPC campaigns, it's usually best not to add broad match keywords because they target a broad range of searches, and some may not be relevant.

This is mainly because building a comprehensive list of negative keywords takes a while and you need them to block all irrelevant searches.

It's best to start with phrase, exact or modified broad match keywords. They allow you to control the types of searches you get while you build your negative list.

When you've built a good list of negative keywords, you can now look to increase your reach by targeting many long tail keywords with broad match type keywords.

How to get 10/10 quality scores

Having keywords with 10/10 quality scores is usually a sign of a well-managed campaign. This shows that ads are targeted to people's searches and are closely related to the keywords in the search campaign.

Quality scores are like the dashboard in your car. The purpose of the dashboard is to alert you to any problem with the engine, tires, lights, or anything else related to your car. It won't fix the problem, but it will reveal what needs to be fixed, so the quality score is just an indicator. It's not the most important metric in your account, however it alerts you to any potential problems and what you can do about them.

There are three main factors that affect your quality scores. These can each have one of three statuses: below average, average, and above average. Improving these factors and bringing them all up to 'above average' status will help you achieve 10/10 quality scores.

Here are some tips on how to do this:

Improve expected click through rate (CTR)

Expected CTR is a prediction of what the CTR will be based on past performance, search term, location, device used and other factors, so it's important that you create targeted ads for your keywords.

For an expected CTR of below average or average, you should look at the various factors to improve it.

Improving the CTR metric will bring your keywords closer to a 10/10 score. This is mainly because CTR is an important quality score factor.

Several ways to improve CTR include:

- Remove poor performing search terms
- Add negative keywords
- Update text ads based on performance
- Create tightly themed ad groups
- Allow Google Ads to automatically show the best performing ads

Improve ad relevance

Ad relevance is one of the most important quality score factors. It's an indication of how targeted your ads are to a visitor's search term.

One way to make your ads relevant is by including the keyword in the ad. People are more likely to click through when they see the words they've used in the ad. They'll perceive your ads as being relevant.

Also, use dynamic keyword insertion (DKI) in the headline of your ad. DKI is a syntax that's used to update the ads dynamically by adding the keyword that has been used. This is an example of DKI:

{KeyWord:Google Ads Specialist}

The keyword 'Google Ads Specialist' is the default text, and this is changed to include the keyword that the searcher has used to find your ad.

This makes adding keywords in the ad a lot easier, especially if you have 10 or more keywords in an ad group.

Improve landing page experience

It's not enough that your ads are relevant to searches. The visitor experience and journey on the page should be high quality, and visitors should be able to find what they're looking for within one click.

Your pages should also include your main keywords in the text. This helps with conversions as people find what they've searched for. They will then click one of your calls to action and make a purchase or signup or whatever other action you require.

Bounce rate also affects the landing page experience factors. People who reach your landing page and leave without viewing other pages are not engaged, so if someone views one page and leaves, that is a 100% bounce rate. You should aim for a bounce rate lower than 50% for all your ad campaigns.

Add ad extensions

Ad extensions help your ads stand out in the auction results. They appear under the normal text ads and highlight other areas of your business. Some important ad extensions to add are sitelinks, callouts, and call extensions.

By adding these, your ads become more relevant to searchers. They're therefore more likely to find what they want and click through to your website.

This helps to boost factors such as ad relevance and expected CTR and therefore improves your quality scores.

Try to add as many ad extensions as possible. That includes location extensions, more callouts, price extensions, all applicable sitelinks, etc.

Remove low performing search terms

Search terms with low CTRs usually underperform for other metrics like conversion rate. These searches lower your quality scores and prevent your campaigns from reaching their potential.

Will paused keywords affect quality scores?

The answer to that is **no**. Each keyword has its own quality scores, and this is calculated when the ad is eligible to run.

There's a misconception that accounts, campaigns, and ad groups have quality scores. This is incorrect. Quality scores are a keyword metric which shows how they're performing for:

- Landing page experience
- Expected click through rate
- Ad relevance

These three factors affect your quality scores. It's calculated each time your ad is eligible to appear in the auction, so it's calculated at auction time and not before or after.

When you first set up your Google Ads campaign, you'll notice that your keywords have no quality score. This is because they have not appeared in any auction result and therefore it cannot be calculated.

Paused keywords may have a historic quality score, but that will have no significance because they're no longer running. The quality score cannot be recalculated when they're paused and will therefore not be updated. They will also not affect your account's performance as long as they remain paused.

CHAPTER 11

Remarketing

Over 90% of people that visit your website will leave, never return, and will forget about your business. You can remind them about your offers through remarketing and bring them back to the website.

The conversion rate for this can be amazing. It's important to set it up as soon as possible and there are tools in Google Ads that help you to set up remarketing.

Audience manager is available in your Google Ads account and is the home of your audience lists, audience sources and audience insights. The benefits of using audience manager are:

1. Set up your audience sources such as the Google Ads tag, analytics app provider or YouTube channel.

2. Create as many audience lists as you like or that make sense for your business based on the audience sources that you've created.

3. You can learn more about the audiences that make up your remarketing lists, such as their interests, demographics, locations, and devices.

Here's what's included in each:

Audience sources

To get started with Google Ads in the new interface, you'll add sources of the first-party data into Audience Sources. These sources help you to then create your remarketing lists that you'll advertise to.

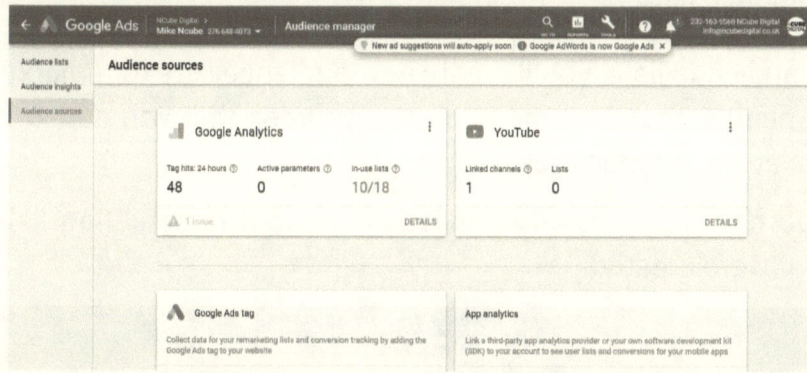

The following audience sources can be added:

Google Ads tag

You collect data from your website to remarket to people who've visited your website.

Google Analytics

Import audiences that you created in your linked Google Analytics account. You can remarket to these audiences with Google Ads.

YouTube

Remarket to people who've seen your videos or channels on YouTube. Track what people do after watching your videos and drive traffic with call-to-action (CTA) overlays.

Customer Data

Upload customer data, like customer contact information, to remarket to them while they browse across Google sites like Google Search, YouTube, and Gmail.

Audience lists

In audience lists, you'll create new audience lists to remarket to people based on the audience sources that you added in the audience manager.

You can also see any previously created remarketing lists that were created.

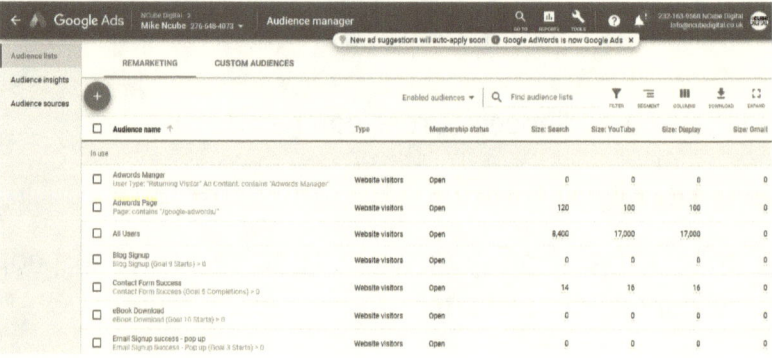

Audience Insights

Audience insights is where you get to understand your audience members and recognise key patterns and recommendations. It breaks down your audiences in your remarketing lists by gender, geography, in-market categories, devices and more.

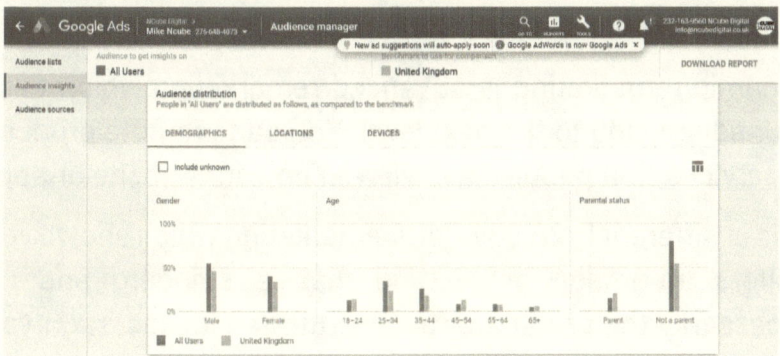

Audience insights provide great insights that can be turned into practical campaign decisions to help you target and attract new people or optimise your ads.

Which advanced remarketing services to set up

Setting up remarketing in Google Ads is a way to show ads to people who've visited your website or mobile phone app in the past. Over 90% of people that come to your website will leave and never return, so it makes sense to have a plan to bring them back.

With advanced remarketing services, you can make that happen. You can target people that arrived but did not purchase. You reconnect with them by showing relevant ads across their different devices.

Here are some advanced remarketing services you should setup:

Dynamic remarketing

Dynamic remarketing is advanced remarketing which takes your advertising to the next level. You can promote products or services that people have viewed on your website or app.

This is different from standard remarketing which shows your visitors an image or text ad that is standard and not necessarily the product or service they've looked at on your website or app.

With dynamic remarketing, prices and offers in ads are updated automatically as you update your products or services. So, people get accurate information and that leads to higher conversions.

Remarketing lists for search ads (RLSA)

With this option, you get to show your ads to past visitors as they make follow up searches on Google. This is when they've been to your website before after having clicked on one of your text ads.

YouTube remarketing

With video remarketing you show your ads to people who have interacted with your YouTube videos or channels. This is a powerful way to increase brand awareness for your business and YouTube channel.

Like other advanced remarketing services, most people who view your videos will leave and never return if you don't retarget them with relevant ads. By reinforcing your message with visitors that have seen your channel and videos, you're more likely to see an increased return on investment.

How to setup PPC remarketing

Setting up a PPC remarketing campaign in Google Ads can feel like a big challenge. This is because of the various steps that you need to take before launching.

However, remarketing can be one of the fastest campaign types to set up. In fact, you can set it up within 30 minutes if you have your image ads ready.

Other campaign types like 'Search' require keyword research first. This can take up a lot of time, whereas remarketing can be set up with one audience to get you started, and you can do this in minutes.

Here are the steps to set up PPC Remarketing:

Link Google Ads & Analytics

The first step to getting standard remarketing working is to link your Google Ads and Analytics account. You will do this in both accounts. Ideally, these should share the same email account to simplify the linking, but you can still do it if they have separate emails.

To link it in Analytics, click the 'Admin' tab. You'll then see three sections with different options under each.

The one you want to look under is 'Property', which is the middle section, and you can find the Google Ads linking option there. When you click on that, it will show you the available Google Ads Customer ID that you can link with.

Google Ads Management

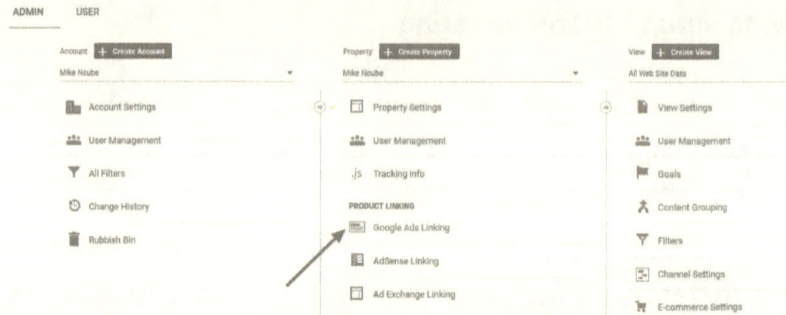

You'll need to have 'Edit' permissions to be able to link accounts.

Next, you should login to your Google Ads account and click on the 'Linked Accounts' section to get to Analytics linking.

You'll see that it's linked now, but you'll need to import the metrics to have full access linking. This will import such essential metrics such as bounce rate.

Create an audience in Analytics

Audiences are the groups of people that you want to target. They are your target market, and they are segmented according to how they've interacted with your website in the past.

You segment your website visitors into different audiences such as:

- Pages they've visited on your website
- How long they've been on the website (e.g., spent 5+ minutes)
- Specific demographics (age, gender, etc.)
- Where they are based

- What devices they've used
- What actions they've performed on the website
- Which call to actions they've completed
- And many others

In fact, there are thousands of audiences you can create in Analytics.

However, there are rules around audiences. The most important is that an audience should have at least 100 members for it to be eligible to run.

When you create your audiences, they'll be automatically available for use in Google Ads. You can see these audiences in 'Shared Library' > 'Audiences' in your Google Ads Account.

To create your audiences in Google Analytics, go to 'Admin" and go to the 'Property' section as I mentioned above regarding linking the accounts. You then click audiences and set up your first list.

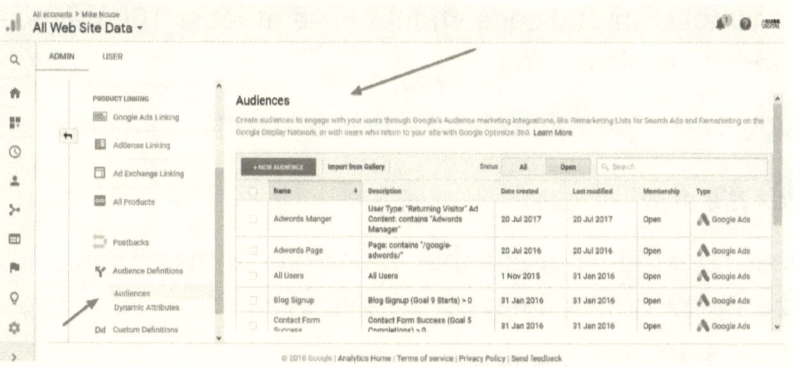

You will state how long you want people to remain in your audience list. The default is 30 days, but you can increase or decrease that according to your requirements.

For example, an emergency service should have a short cookie length. Maybe a maximum of a few days. People are unlikely to be still looking for that many days later, so it has a short life span.

If you're an online retailer of clothing, you can afford to have a longer cookie length. Maybe start with 180 days to keep people remarketed to for a longer time as they shop around.

Create new image ads

Next, create the image ads that your target audiences will see. Remember these should be relevant to the specific audiences you have. For example, if you want to target people that have purchased in the past, the messages should be different for people that visited but did not purchase.

These image ads will appear on third party websites that are part of the Google Display Network. So, as your past visitors visit other websites, they'll see your ads and that will encourage them to return.

Remember, an audience should have at least 100 members before its eligible to run.

Google also has rules about image ad formats, and they are:

Max file size

Make sure that your ads that are no bigger than 150KB in file size. Below are the images sizes you can use in pixels:

- 250 x 250 – Square
- 200 x 200 – Small square
- 468 x 60 – Banner

- 728 x 90 – Leaderboard
- 300 x 250 – In-line rectangle
- 336 x 280 – Large rectangle
- 120 x 600 – Skyscraper
- 160 x 600 – Wide skyscraper
- 300 x 600 – Half-page ad
- 970 x 90 – Large leaderboard

Create a PPC remarketing campaign

Finally, you can set up the campaign in Google Ads. The type of campaign you'll set up, in this case, to advertise with image display ads, is a Display Network Only campaign.

This will be different from a remarketing list for search ads (RLSA) which retargets people that are searching on Google.

Your PPC remarketing campaign will have various ad groups. Each will be based on one or more of your audiences.

In campaign settings, make sure you put a cap on how many times people will see your images. You don't want them to feel like they are being followed and hounded as they browse the web. You could put an impression cap of five per day.

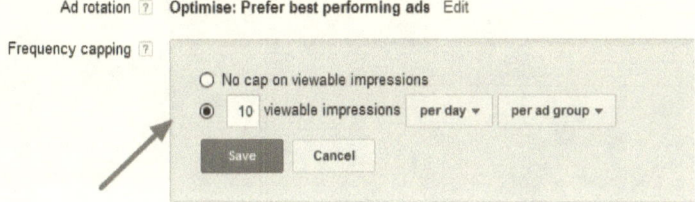

Conclusion

I'm confident these resources and tips will help you to manage Google Ads and run a profitable account.

We've covered the main factors of running and optimising campaigns in Google Ads so you can get the best results from them and not waste your budget.

This includes basic monitoring of your campaigns and ongoing optimisation that ensures you're achieving the goals that you've set for your business in Google Ads.

We have also had a look at more advanced features like bid strategy selection which helps you to set bids at auction-time or bid manually at the keyword-level and have more control.

Resources

There are many resources that will help you to run effective PPC campaigns in Google Ads. Check these out:

PPC Courses - https://ppcuniversity.mikencube.co.uk/

Visit the PPC University to sign up to free courses to learn about PPC and Google Ads advertising. You will learn how to set up and manage effective campaigns.

Google Skill Shop - https://skillshop.withgoogle.com/

This is the official Google training platform that offers free courses in a Learning Management System (LMS). You can take the exams, and if you pass, you will be certified and can work towards Google Partner status.

Google Ads Blog - https://www.mikencube.co.uk/blog/

Check out my blog to learn effective strategies and tips on how to manage your campaigns effectively. Sign up to get regular updates in your inbox.

Google Ads Academy - https://googleadsacademy.mikencube.co.uk/

Get a full day online training session, either one-to-one or in a group, to equip you with all you need to run great campaigns without spending a penny at the Google Ads Academy.

PPC Tutor Podcast - https://ppctutorpodcast.mikencube.co.uk/

Follow the PPC Tutor Podcast to get the latest tips and resources you need to run effective PPC campaigns in Google Ads, and to find out the best way for you to learn about PPC.

PPC Webinars - http://ppcwebinars.mikencube.co.uk/

Join free webinars each month to learn about Google Ads and get actionable insights that you can implement in your own campaigns.

About The Author

Mike Ncube is a leading Google Ads specialist with over 13 years' experience working with businesses around the world where he has set up and managed targeted pay per click (PPC) campaigns.

Mike is a speaker, author, mentor, and trainer and is always ready to help anyone looking to get started in the industry or needs helps with their campaigns.

www.ingramcontent.com/pod-product-compliance
Lightning Source LLC
Chambersburg PA
CBHW030949180526
45163CB00002B/713